COUPLES COMMUNICATION WORKBOOK

A Couple's Intimacy Workbook with 10 Steps for Conflict Resolution, 100 Questions, Exercises, and Quizzes to Develop a Deeper Physical and Emotional Intimacy

MONICA TRAVIS

Copyright - 2021 -

All rights reserved.

The content contained within this book may not be reproduced, duplicated or transmitted without direct written permission from the author or the publisher.

Under no circumstances will any blame or legal responsibility be held against the publisher, or author, for any damages, reparation, or monetary loss due to the information contained within this book, either directly or indirectly.

Legal Notice:

This book is copyright protected. It is only for personal use. You cannot amend, distribute, sell, use, quote or paraphrase any part, or the content within this book, without the consent of the author or publisher.

Disclaimer Notice:

Please note the information contained within this document is for educational and entertainment purposes only. All effort has been executed to present accurate, up to date, reliable, complete information. No warranties of any kind are declared or implied. Readers acknowledge that the author is not engaged in the rendering of legal, financial, medical or professional advice. The content within this book has been derived from various sources. Please consult a licensed professional before attempting any techniques outlined in this book.

By reading this document, the reader agrees that under no circumstances is the author responsible for any losses, direct or indirect, that are incurred as a result of the use of the information contained within this document, including, but not limited to, errors, omissions, or inaccuracies.

TABLE OF CONTENTS

INTRODUCTION — 7

Chapter 1
COMMUNICATION IS KEY — 11
Communication Is Key: Steps and Guidelines — 13
Summary — 22

Chapter 2
REMOVING GENDER STEREOTYPES — 25
Are You in a Gender Stereotyping Relationship? — 26
Summary — 33

Chapter 3
THIS IS A TWO WAY THING — 35
Sign 1: Effort Is Becoming an Effort — 36
Sign 2: Your Time Is Spent Elsewhere — 38
Sign 3: No Longer Making the Time — 39
Sign 4: The Small Things Stop — 40
Sign 5: On Different Pages — 42
Sign 6: Looking for Conflict — 43
Summary — 45

Chapter 4
LET'S GET PHYSICAL — 47
Step 1: Understanding Each Other's Body Language — 49
Step 2: A Healthy Sex Life — 50
Step 3: Have Joint Body Goals — 52
Step 4: The Comfort and Happiness of Touch — 53
Step 5: It's Okay to Have Boundaries — 54
Step 6: Maintain Steps 1 to 5 — 55
Summary — 57

Chapter 5
MENTAL STIMULATION — 59
What Is the Purpose of Mental Stimulation — 60
Find Your Common Interests — 61
Mental Stimulation Is Good for Your Health — 64
Summary — 66

TABLE OF CONTENTS

Chapter 6
CONFLICT AND TRUST RESOLUTION — 69
Conflict Resolution Steps — 70
Trust Resolution — 74
Combine Conflict and Trust Steps — 77
Summary — 79

Chapter 7
APPRECIATE THE DIFFERENCES — 81
Difference of Opinion — 82
Difference in Personality — 84
Insecurities — 85
Life and Cultural Differences — 87
Summary — 88

Chapter 8
NEVER COMPARE AND ACCEPTING THE WRONG — 91
No One Is Perfect — 92
Some People Apologize Differently — 93
Focus on the Good — 94
Give Each Other Time — 95
You Can Ask for Help Collectively — 96
Summary — 97

Chapter 9
COUPLE GOALS — 99
Importance of Setting Goals — 100
Summary — 106

Chapter 10
EXERCISES AND QUESTIONS TO PROMOTE A HEALTHY RELATIONSHIP — 109
Connection — 110

Chapter 11
40 QUIZZES TO DEVELOP A DEEPER EMOTIONAL AND PHYSICAL INTIMACY — 171
The Match Game — 171
The Bedroom Quiz — 173

TABLE OF CONTENTS

Deal or No Deal	175
How Do You Love? Physical Intimacy	176
How Do You Love? Encouraging Words	177
How Do You Love? A Helping Hand	178
How Do You Love? Alone Time	179
How Do You Love? Making Purchases	180
Are You Passionate?	181
Find out if you are a passionate couple! You get one point for every "YES" answer.	181
Which Kink Should You Try in the Bedroom?	182
Is Romance Alive in Your Relationship?	183
Is Your Partner Your Best Friend?	184
Should You Change Your Relationship?	185
How to Improve Your Relationship	186
Is Your Intimacy Enough?	187
Do You Trust Your Partner?	188
Will You Be Together Forever?	189
Are You and Your Partner a Good Match?	190
Is Your Relationship Healthy?	191
The Favorites Quiz	192
A Random Assortment	193
Are You an Introverted Couple?	194
Are You an Extroverted Couple?	195
The Conflict Resolution Quiz	196
Do You Appreciate Your Partner Enough?	197
Do You Make Your Partner Happy?	198
What Should You Add to Your Relationship?	199
Are You Couple Goals?	200
How Can You Help Your Relationship Grow?	201
How Great Are You at Being in a Relationship?	203
Are Your Communication Skills Good Enough?	204
Can You Handle Your Jealousy?	205
Do You Believe That Your Partner Finds You Attractive?	206
Are You Ready for Kids?	207
Should You Get a Pet Together?	208
Should You Spend More Time Together?	209
Is the Sex Hot Enough?	210
Should You Kiss More?	211
Do You Turn Your Partner On?	212
What Should You Do for Date Night?	213
CONCLUSION	215
REFERENCES	219

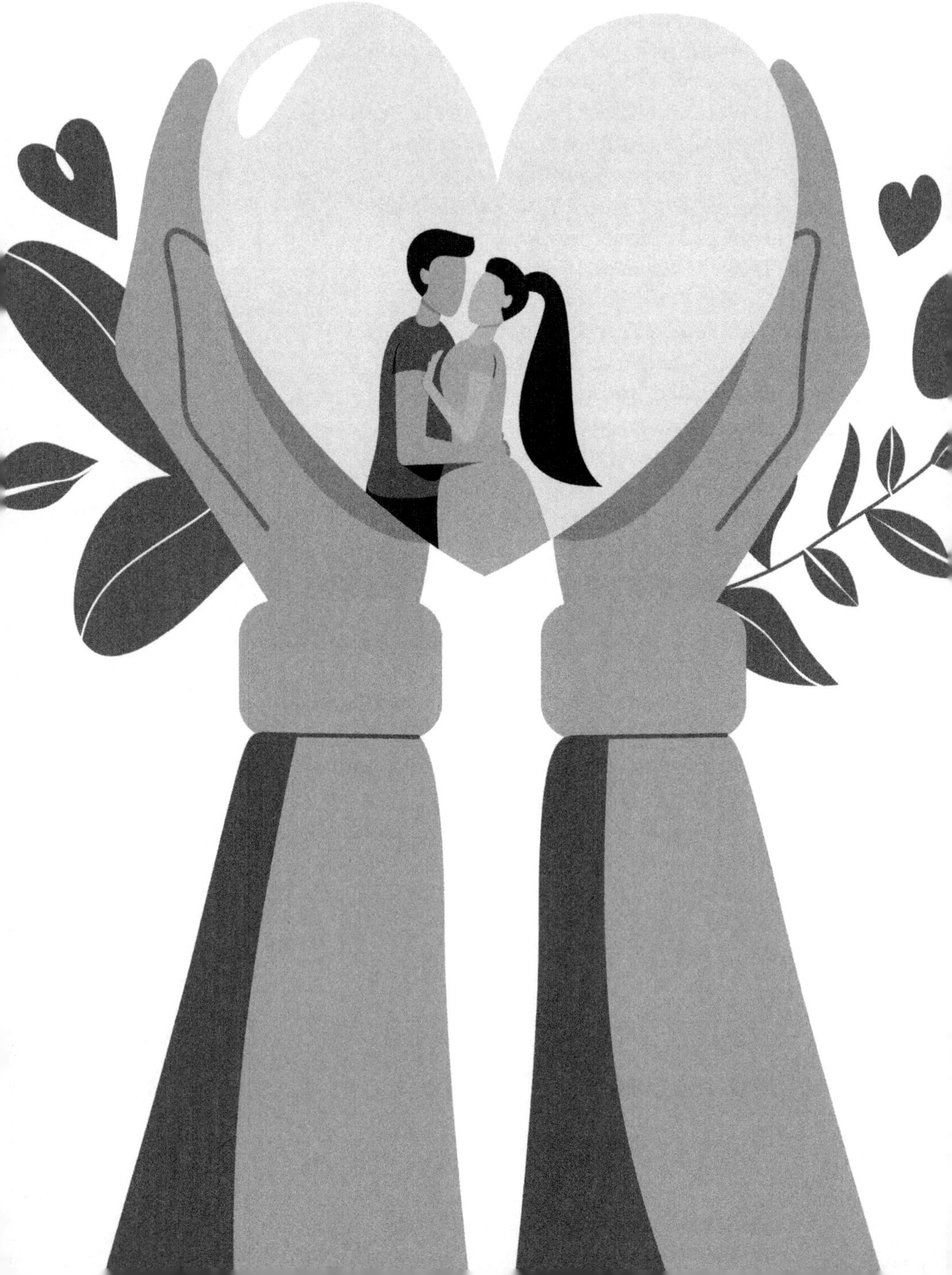

Introduction

"At your absolute best, you still won't be good enough for the wrong person. At your worst, you'll still be worth it to the right person" **(Salmansohn, n.d.).**

It's not uncommon for couples to go through rough spells and question the foundations of the relationship they are in. We are all humans and there is no such thing as the perfect relationship without any difficulties along the way that will test your boundaries in a relationship. If anything, the key and happiness in a successful couple's relationship are how well they deal with problems that test their compatibility with each other. This workbook aims to provide you with an eleven-chapter guide on how to manage those problems that test the fragility of a couple's relationship successfully, and how to strengthen the relationship for any further problems in the future.

This book will teach you chapter by chapter the common core fundamentals to help you bring back your relationship to its best again. Each chapter applies to both men and women as equals and will always emphasize this throughout the book, as this is still a common issue that couples can fail to grasp. You will be taught and given the necessary guides on the important facets of communication both verbally and physically, as no relationship—whether couples, friends, or family—can last without the essentials of communication. These steps will guide you in a way applicable to all general situations and problems but may not necessarily apply to you at the moment of reading. Therefore, it's important to note that you can always come back and refer to the workbook, as it will surely cover whatever difficulty you may be going through as a couple. A modern couple's intimacy book requires modern solutions and guides. All the chapters in this book apply to the 21st-century couple, as relationship dynamics have drastically changed over the last few decades, especially when it comes to gender roles.

You will also be shown throughout the chapters, some reasons you may not have even thought of that are causing problems in your relationship. More than this, you may not even realize you had before you started reading this book. Most couple's intimacy books try to focus on one or two particular aspects of a relationship to solve all the problems in the present and future. This workbook will guide you on all aspects of not just solving common and new types of problems, but also how to keep the relationship going strong to either avoid it in the future or stop it completely altogether. This workbook will not stray away from educating and helping you with the more intimate parts of your relationship or "bedroom advice" as some might say. Always keep in mind that each chapter is aimed at covering the broader scale of issues in simple terms and in as much detail as possible. The aim will be that you can use these steps and guides in each chapter to apply them to you personally as a couple in the most comfortable way for both of you. This means that you can have a more in-depth and personal attachment to what you have to do and therefore have a permanent subconscious imprint on both you and your partner in your relationship that you will never forget—but the book is always there as a refresher.

As this workbook is a modern guide for the 21st century, it applies to couples of all walks of life, as the problems are ones that will generally be encountered that you may or may not have known. So if you are a same-sex couple, an interracial couple, and so on, this book applies to you as much as the next couple having issues. This workbook is gender-neutral and therefore all parties in the relationship are on equal playing fields, as you will see emphasized in each chapter—because no one person in a couple is more important than the other. There are many couples books out there that like to focus on one particular gender in a relationship, which often creates further issues and deviates from the equality that all relationships should critically have. So no matter what you look like or who you are, if you are having problems in your relationship within reason, this book has been written for you. The idea for every chapter is not only personal experience, but it should also be relatable to the problem you are having in your relationship.

The objective of this book is to leave you with a healthy understanding, as well as a written friend that can help you through the trials and tribulations—which you can always come back to—as you grow in strength in your relationship. As much as this is a workbook to help you with the problems and build on the strengths of your relationship, this is also a book you and your significant other can read and enjoy about parts of your relationship you didn't know you had. Enjoy the workbook, because it's written to bring back joy to something you and your significant other cherish for as long as you are together. You or both of you are taking the necessary steps and effort to make your relationship the best it can be but remember that no relationship is perfect.

Chapter 1
COMMUNICATION IS KEY

"The way we communicate with others and with ourselves ultimately determines the quality of our lives"
(A Quote about Communication, 2015).

Communication is an essential part of everything we do as humans, whether we verbally say something, communicate with our body or sometimes not say or do anything at all. It forms one of the key pillars of any and every single relationship you can think of and is quite literally what makes the world tick every day. Therefore it can be argued that communication is the most critical aspect in the relationship of a couple because without it you would have not been in a relationship, to begin with. So, if communication is so obviously important, why does it continue to be one of the most common recurring problems amongst couples around the world? Well, it generally has to do with either how we communicate, how others understand and sometimes that we do not communicate at all. Every individual is unique and may interpret or understand things differently, but people also change and thus changes the way they communicate.

The same goes for you and your significant other, your way of communication is different from other people, but will also change over the weeks, months and years you have a couple. Though the one thing that tends to stay the same between you and your partner is each other's values and therefore commonality in communication can always be found there. This is something that is commonly forgotten in couples as they get comfortable with each other. In the beginning stage between two people, infatuation drives that effort for one another and later when you get comfortable with each other, that effort and subsequent communication dwindles. This chapter then focuses on how to rekindle that communication from the infatuation phase, because let's face it, that's when you could not wait to see and talk to each other. The steps provided to you will cover broader situations that encapsulate multiple problems couples face with regard to communication so that you can use the steps to help you in any issue of communication you are having in your relationship.

Other than helping you as a couple, these six steps will also help you with interactions with others within your circle, who—as discussed in later chapters—have an impact on the dynamics of your relationship. We can then sort of "kill two birds with one stone" which makes chapters later come easier to follow and relatable.

COMMUNICATION IS KEY: STEPS AND GUIDELINES

These steps will form the foundation of everything you will use going forward in your communication skills or for the future of your relationship.

Communication is an essential piece for any problem to be solved as a couple, but it has to be initiated together and the effort must be put in to communicate in a manner that is correct. These steps will teach you that and help you identify present and future communication blocks you may encounter as a couple. Remember that communication issues among couples are a usual thing that happens at some point in time. Nobody is a perfect communicator and you will not always understand your partner, otherwise, all relationships would be perfect right? Also, another important point to take note of is that one of the most rewarding things as a couple is solving problems together which will only serve to strengthen your relationship.

Step 1: Is Communication the Actual Problem?

This may sound obvious, but sometimes the lack of communication between you or your partner may not be the actual problem. There may be another underlying factor that you or your partner is hiding that is causing difficulties to communicate. This may also seem confusing because people don't communicate when there is a problem. However, we are focusing on why communication has withered because of the lack of need to communicate anymore. Often when couples are in a relationship for an extended period of time, the communication between the two lessens. Initially, this is not an issue but becomes an issue eventually when either person starts benefiting negatively from it. This is where understanding if communication is a problem, to begin with, comes into play. Thus that negative benefit is the underlying problem that originally came from the lack of communication that was not a problem initially and now has become one because of something else. Thus you have to tackle the underlying problem, then tackle the lack of communication that leads to it.

For example, you are a couple that is past the phase of infatuation and is now comfortable enough with each other to do those things you once considered embarrassing in front of each other. Now that you know everything about each other's lives, the communication between the two of you has become much less frequent. This initially was not a problem as both of you become accustomed to each other's everyday rituals and there was nothing to worry about or speak about. One day something breaks the two of you out of this routine and becomes a problem both of you never encountered. Usually, if you know each other well enough, this may not become an issue, though, on the flip side, it may be something that can make or break the relationship. This problem, therefore, came about because of the original lack of communication and turned into something else entirely. The difference is seen from when you first started dating, to where you are now as a steady-is couple. Couples sometimes forget that they solved problems better at the beginning of their relationship because of their dynamic communication than they do when they get comfortable with each other.

The more you communicate the fewer problems you encounter, even if you have been with someone for the most part of your life. Once it starts dwindling, other problems are caused because of it, and then it just compounds one after the other.

Step 2: Understanding Each Other

Even though the more we communicate the fewer problems we have, we need to understand the person we are communicating with or listening to. If everyone communicated the same way, there would be no need to write this chapter and you would not be having any problems with your partner. As a couple, you communicate differently than you do with other people, and it's important you stick to that communication that yields the best results. Have you ever encountered a scenario where you are trying to explain something to someone, only to make the situation worse? The same can be applied to couples; you will encounter problems that make each other communicate differently. This also revolves around sensitive topics, such as family, sex, and each other. You are constantly learning and growing from each other, and therefore topics become more sensitive as time goes on. Understanding and communicating with someone the wrong way can easily ruin a relationship; it can give the other person an idea that you cannot handle a serious crisis—especially if they are involved in it.

Understanding how to communicate with your partner also provides comfort to them. It builds trust that they can talk to you about anything and everything without hesitation. There are many couples that are in a relationship but still cannot talk to each other about certain things out of discomfort. This is not to be confused with keeping secrets, rather than the one person or both not being able to comfortably communicate something sensitive to the other. However, putting in the communicative effort to understand your partner can only do nothing but good for your relationship in both the short and long term. Take your time because not everyone is an open book; some people take longer than others to communicate everything about themselves—communication is a two-way street.

Step 3: Don't Make It Public

People often communicate with others around them when they are going through problems. As a couple, you may have close friends outside the relationship who you seek advice from because it's not necessarily a bad idea to get a neutral or second opinion from a reliable source. Even though it's not a bad thing, try to keep it to a minimum, because as a couple, it's best to communicate problems with each other to each other. If you are going to seek advice from another person, make sure that the tail is not carried to another person, and eventually, everyone knows about the problems you have been having. Lastly, never post about it on any form of social media, even if you keep it in a sort of riddle-like many people do. What this does is either make you look like an attention seeker, you start getting advice from the wrong people, you embarrass your partner, and most likely cripple any form of sensitive or serious communication as a couple. This may not seem like something that applies to you, but anger and the right timing can make people do hurtful things with words.

If you are in a relationship with someone who prefers to discuss issues with other people—as hard as this may sound—you should put in the effort if you genuinely love the person to communicate with each other. The golden rule is that successful relationships are built upon good communication with each other. If your partner shares the same feelings back, the favor will be returned eventually.

This also relates to the step Understanding Each Other. By keeping the communication away from others, you build upon the strength of communication with each other.

Step 4: Always Be Honest in Communication

This step is crucial because a little lie can go a long way to ruining a relationship. There is a saying that if you don't have anything good to say, you should not say it. This is not the best way to go about things as a couple. Yes, there is a fine line between hurting your partner's feelings and doing the right thing, but it comes down to trust. Being honest about everything you communicate should always be a staple among couples; the person is with you for who you are, and it should always stay that way. On the other hand, never feel ashamed to give your significant other honest communication that may cause a negative situation. The reason is then you can sort out that problem at once and not have to worry about it boiling inside of you, and later coming up with unnecessary exaggeration and emotion. This—down the line—will only make communication easier with each other and will make problem-solving much easier.

What are the consequences of lying? Well honestly, you may get away with it in the beginning, but it will eventually catch up with you as all lies do. This cannot be stressed enough but consistently communicating lies in a relationship will break it eventually. It may have been something you used at the start of your relationship, but if you want to keep it long-term, your partner needs to know who you are as well as all your honest opinions. You truly get to know someone once you communicate honestly with each other. It may be something that happens over time, but that is part of the journey as a couple. Though you may not like communicating something negative to your partner, don't be afraid to give them the bad news that concerns you. You open up to them about your own insecurities, bad habits, and even lies may pave the way for them to comfortably communicate it back to you. If they want to be in a relationship with you, they will be there through those tough times and communicate it too. Here's a side note, if you are a couple who is looking to get married, having a communication session of honesty is something that can help your relationship significantly and make it all that much stronger with that person.

Step 5: Don't Be Afraid to Fight, but Keep It Verbal

Many couples try to avoid negative confrontation, but in fact, this is something that can be considered positive confrontation. Fighting often brings out the honesty in someone with regard to someone else or the situation. Having a verbal disagreement about something brings positive results if you are both willing to listen to each other's opinions. The honesty that comes from it and the willingness to equally listen to each other's opinions regarding something negative will strengthen your relationship and love for each other in tough times. Avoid fighting in a relationship and you will find that in tough times as a couple, you won't be able to cope as a couple because you refuse to tackle issues and let them simmer over time. The answer is simple: fight with each other verbally. It may be borderline verbal abuse, but you will come out of it a stronger couple should you choose to work together. The golden rule for this step is that fighting amongst a couple should never become physical. That is considered abuse and should never in any circumstances be the appropriate solution. Keep it verbal and honest. You know you are right for each other when you work it out.

Verbally fighting also allows couples to vent necessary frustration that may come from other factors outside of their relationship, such as work, family, and friends. Therefore, both of you are simultaneously solving many problems where you just needed someone to vent or to. Verbally fighting should never lead to the end of a relationship of a couple unless it's about something where one of you seriously compromised the relationship, such as proof of having an affair for example. Other than that, fighting within reason is healthy and should only strengthen you if you are with the right person in a relationship. If you feel you are fighting too much with your partner, consider the reasons you are having to. It should be reasons that condone such verbal disagreements which are usually very sensitive or personal topics; don't mistake it for simple debate disagreements. If you feel that you as a couple are fighting about reasons that are insignificant, remember the step about understanding your partner. Your partner may find some things more important than you and it's important to understand that. Also, avoid written communication when fighting. This may give an indication that you are not taking the issue seriously or you may be afraid of verbalizing your opinions and speaking face to face.

Step 6: There Is a Time and Place to Appropriately Talk

Sometimes communicating with each other about certain things needs to be timed well. This is not lying to your partner but rather waiting for the appropriate time to tell them something. For example, if your partner is at a funeral for someone significant in their life, they would not want to hear more bad news. If communication on something important can wait during a sensitive time, rather communicate it when the appropriate time comes. If you are fighting about something, refrain from verbally voicing it in front of other people, especially if it's something serious. You should keep it for the drive back home or wait until both of you are alone and physically present. Face-to-face communication is the best form of communication as a couple because you see the emotion of the person that you will never get over the phone or through written communication. Only ever fight in front of people you really trust and if it's really necessary to do so for that moment, wait for the appropriate time and place if you both can.

Taking the appropriate times to communicate with your partner can only give positive results to both parties involved. It saves the possible embarrassment and uncomfortable scenario of fighting in front of people and can be worse when it's in front of family because they may want to get involved or they may spread to other members of the family. In the future, your partner will also consider your feelings if the same scenario happens to them, which once again will only build your relationship and strengthen it. The golden rule for this step can be that any topic that is considered sensitive, personal, or inappropriate to or about your partner should be discussed behind closed doors as a couple. It's important to have each other's back, even in times that are negative as a couple.

SUMMARY

What should you have learned from this chapter? It's learning whether the communication is the actual problem you are having as a couple. There are ways in which you can identify it and it might have even been the root cause of your future problems as a subsequent run-off effect. The next thing that was discussed was understanding how to communicate as a couple because not everyone has the same or shared understanding of a situation. This chapter highlighted the importance of understanding your partner as it will make communication for both of you easier in the present and the future. This was then moved to why making your couple's communication public is a bad idea. It's best to communicate—especially on sensitive or personal topics—between you and your partner as a couple, though it's not necessarily a bad thing to get an opinion from someone you trust. The next point was the critical form of communication and always being honest with each other. The reason? Lying can easily break a relationship because of how long it can take for someone to trust another person they have an intimate attachment.

This chapter touched on the topic that many couples avoid, the positivity of verbally fighting with each other within reason. Combine this with understanding your partner and fighting can strengthen a relationship in the toughest of times or can prepare a couple for tough times, which highlights that fighting is not necessarily a bad thing with the right person and the positivity it can bring when done in the appropriate manner in the final step. As a couple, there is a time and place to sometimes communicate with each other on certain things. Constant communication is good amongst a couple. Sharing certain things at the right moment can say a lot about you and in turn, reflect positively on your significant other who should return the favor. Overall, chapter one covers arguably the most important part of communication in relationships and is the foundation of the chapters to come. Therefore, with core communication established, you can move forward to tackling further issues in your relationship.

Thanks again for choosing this book, make sure to leave a short review on Amazon if you enjoy it. I'd really love to hear your thoughts.

Chapter 2
REMOVING GENDER STEREOTYPES

"Men learn to love the woman they are attracted to. Women learn to become attracted to the man they fall in love with" **(Gender Stereotyping Quotes, n.d.).**

The only difference between a man and a woman in a relationship is their physical features. Other than that they are seen as equals and as a couple; you should always treat each other this way. Even though we are in the 21st century, men's and women's gender roles are still very prevalent in today's society amongst couples. Men still have this idea of being the dominant individual and primary breadwinner of the house, while women are trying to break down that barrier for themselves, although some still feel the man should be the breadwinner. Stereotypes are something rarely talked about in relationships because they are often overshadowed by something else or because it's modern society—so no one thinks about it in a relationship setting but rather in a corporate setting. However, subconsciously a couple, may not realize that the cause of their problems and unhappiness is linked to gender stereotypes, but rather to a much more direct problem.

Stereotypes amongst couples are also something that's not really communicated because once you fall into the routine with each other it almost becomes oblivious between two people. Stereotypes in a relationship are one of those hidden problems you must tackle together. Identifying them is something that can surprise individuals in a relationship and can often disguise itself through one person in the relationship who is putting in more effort than the other. Stereotypes can also easily break relationships through one person expecting something from the other because of the gender roles society deemed for men and women. This chapter seeks to identify whether you or both of you in your relationship are actually stereotyping each other—maybe subconsciously—and it's causing problems.

ARE YOU IN A GENDER STEREOTYPING RELATIONSHIP?

Before you read the steps, do you believe you are judging your partner in a manner that is stereotypical? If not, then what are the reasons you believe you are not? Now compare your reasons to the four steps below and see if you fall into any of these categories. You may not realize that you are subconsciously treating your partner in a certain way and usually for factors you never thought about before. Reverse the questions if you believe your partner is treating you in a way according to gender roles.

You may also feel they are treating you a certain way, but you may also be allowing them to treat you in a certain way. If you are both comfortable with it, then there is not anything to worry about; however, it's still something to think about in the future of your relationship. Always remember, you only truly know someone once you start living with them because you see how they usually act when you are not around versus when you are.

Use these steps to help you identify whether you are in a gender role-run relationship and understand how this is impacting you. You may not realize that it may be the source of your problems in your relationship. Use step one to establish a good foundation of understanding and identify whether these gender roles are affecting your relationship negatively or positively. Sometimes people like to conform to the norms of their gender, and there are many relationships that are successful because each individual sticks to their assigned gender roles. However, this is the modern world of gender identity, and everyone should not be restricted from doing something based on stereotypes.

Step 1: Are You Restricting Each Other?

We have this argument about what women can and can't do and likewise for the men as well. Couples often don't realize they restrict themselves based on their gender but disguise it as a personality trait. As a man or the dominant one in a relationship for same-sex, you may take charge of situations constantly over your partner. Even in same-sex relationships, we see the dominant one as the "manly" one and the other as the more feminine on some occasions. In some relationships, the woman is the dominant one and because of society's gender roles, this can directly affect the confidence a man has in his relationship and even around others. It's something that is constantly overlooked and sometimes coming on too strong reflects badly on your partner as you refuse to let them take the limelight so to speak. Always make sure that in every situation you guys are in you are both on an equal playing field emotionally and in agreement.

Other restricting indicators can be who earns more than the other for a couple. Often more prevalent with men, when the woman is earning more than they are, it tends to affect them negatively rather than motivationally. On the flip side, when the man is earning more in a relationship, he tends to feel like the one with more power and this can work vice versa in today's society. The idea is to not devalue each other but motivate each other to greater heights, especially if one is doing better than the other. Often couples revert to their gender roles when it comes to earning money and it's something that is common in the older generation but should not be taught to the current generation. Here's something to think about: if you are a couple with children, this will reflect on the way you raise your children. Though everyone is different, are you with someone because they provide a specific gender role to you? If so, are you happy with it being that way? If not, did you communicate it to them, and did they understand? The idea of the modern couple is that neither should ever be restricted because of gender stereotyping.

Make a list a couple of all the things you feel conform to stereotyping each other in any restrictive way. Come to a consensus on whether these are problems or might become potential problems. This also creates good debate between you as a couple and can often identify a relationship dynamic you never knew existed. For example, the list could consist of who cooks, who cleans, the effect of your jobs, the effort each other puts in, who takes charge and when, and so on. These may seem like insignificant points, but they will surely improve and strengthen your relationship.

Step 2: Outside Influences and Culture

Family and friends can sometimes influence what you as a man or woman should do when you are in a relationship. They are those trusted advisors that may not be in a relationship themselves, but you trust their opinion through thick and thin. Usually, they would be the first to tell you when they see something wrong and whether that's biased or neutral depends on the person. If you're a man or woman, your male and female friends may influence you in a certain way to act in a relationship, but ultimately you need to understand that you should know who you're with better than anyone else. Unless it's early stages in your relationship, then you should give each other the chance to get to know one another in time. If you are a couple who have not been in a relationship for very long, gender stereotypes will tend to play a role in the beginning until you understand each other on a more personal level—gender roles may gradually swap over time.

One of the most gender-stereotypical influences is culture. People who follow their culture strictly often have strict gender roles they have been raised with, and that gets transferred to their relationships. Clashes often happen when it's two different cultures, or when one individual in a couple doesn't follow the norms of gender roles. Culture is a sensitive topic, to begin with, and adding stereotypes to it can make it even more difficult, especially if an individual was raised a certain way their entire life. However, when you are in a relationship with someone and this problem arises, you need to retrace your steps and figure out why you got into a relationship with this person. Usually, these types of problems are only prevalent after some substantial time in a relationship when you become comfortable and start enforcing things that may make your partner uncomfortable or in this case based on who they are or their gender. Hence, both the list you made in step one would be a good starting point to tackle those problems of culture and influence together.

Step 3: Compromise and Do What's Best for the Relationship

There is no such thing as the perfect relationship because everyone goes through problems—some more serious than others—that you couples have to get through. However, why do some people describe their relationship as perfect? The answer is compromising and doing what is best equally for one another. When two people sacrifice something for the other to be happy, that is one of the pinnacles of trust and love between the two people. How can this relate to gender stereotyping? It's more so from the stereotypes brought on by culture or if individuals in a relationship were raised with gender roles in mind. For example, the man in the relationship wants to be the provider in the relationship but the woman may either earn more than him or also want to support the household financially. The compromise can come from allowing him to be the provider for the house for the sake of pride and happiness of the relationship; however, assuring him that should they go through a bad financial patch, the women can provide. It can also work vice versa which the woman wants to be the provider and that compromise is made. This can also be applied to same-sex couples, where one individual wants to be the dominant mantle in the relationship financially.

Sometimes for the best interest of keeping the relationship strong, you may have to go against certain aspects of your culture that are negatively affecting both of you in a relationship. Many cultures demand the man to be the breadwinner and frown upon women who do not stay at home to cook and raise children. Though that has turned full circle in the world of today and those that come from strict gender role-orientated cultures may find it difficult. However, a constant in every relationship throughout the generations has shown that many couples that compromise and do what's logically best for each other go on to very long and successful relationships. Compromising can be an incredibly difficult thing to do in general, and for a couple, it should only be in the best interest of the relationship and in agreement by both.

Step 4: Promote Independence and Never Control

One way to work around stereotypes in a relationship is to promote independence as a couple. This is not independence as an individual but independence together away from other influences. This is used to strengthen the relationship of a couple such as simply booking a holiday away or spending some time away from family and friends at home. It's a healthy step in general for couples to spend some alone time with each other. This allows couples to get comfortable with each other, possibly in ways they never thought of before, and to be their best free selves, not having to worry about judgment from others because of how they have a relationship. The other aspect of independence individually in a couple is not to control each other, as you do things for each other in a relationship out of love and/or happiness with one another. Usually, when couples are away and alone, the stereotypes move away as you enjoy each other and do not worry about who does this or that or who needs to do certain things in the relationship. This step aims at showing you what happens when you allow the best parts of being with someone who flourishes without anything to influence the relationship. Sometimes the best way to tackle problems as a couple is just to be away from everyone and everything, even the common advice.

SUMMARY

This chapter covers a topic that not many couples actually focus on. Gender stereotyping amongst couples of today is something that is still not as common as it was in the past but is a hidden contributor that affects couples negatively. Often, gender stereotyping is mistaken for other problems a couple faces in their relationship. The steps cover this basis to identify factors that you may be gender stereotyping your partner, but you just don't realize it. The first step revolves around whether you are restricting your partner in any way because of who they are that may relate to their gender. You may not realize it at first, but subconsciously in your mind, it is happening and translating into your behavior. Indicators were discussed that can possibly lead to stereotypical behavior and advised that you as a couple should make a list to narrow down these indicators. The focus was then moved to the outside influences and culture that influence the individuals in a relationship; these influences were identified and whether you listen to these influences or not is entirely up to you. This chapter introduced a sensitive topic on how culture continues to promote gender roles in a relationship and the role it can play for a couple trying to work around it in their relationship.

Step three was a very important step that follows step two about compromising and promoting the best interests of the couple. Thus taking all those outside influences and cultural norms of stereotyping in a relationship and coming to a consensus as a couple. This step is crucial because when a couple starts compromising for each other out of their best interests, this will only further strengthen a relationship by leaps and bounds. Lastly was promoting independence and a couple and blocking out all those negative influences and focusing on each other. Like at the beginning of a relationship, you learn a lot about your partner when just the two of you spend some alone time for extended periods. You then understand them more and the reasoning behind their behavior. In this case, the focus is on stereotypes between each other. You may have been controlling your partner even if your intentions were pure, but it did not affect them in a positive manner from your perspective. Stereotypes amongst couples still exist in a manner that is not as obvious anymore; however, it's still important to be aware if you are unintentionally or intentionally affecting your partner negatively by judging them this way.

Chapter 3
THIS IS A TWO WAY THING

"Love is that condition in which the happiness of another person is essential to your own"
(Inspirational Quotes, n.d.).

A couple's relationship is not something that should be one-sided, and effort should not be put in by one of the two in a relationship. This may sound obvious enough, but individuals in a relationship often don't realize how much effort their partner is putting in towards the relationship or if they are the individual who feels they are putting in the most effort. For a couple to properly function and communicate, both of you need to be on the same page in not only the good but the bad times as well. Chapter one covered the foundation—communication—that you can use to help your relationship become a two-way street. If a person wants to be in a relationship with you, they would equally commit to it as much as you do and vice versa. If both of you are not trying, then the relationship will surely break down and no logical advice will help. There are various signs to look out for like a couple that can lead to this dark road; the idea would be to prevent it before it's too late.

These signs might seem obvious enough, but there is a reason they come up regularly in couple's relationships. These indicators or signs are usually normal stages couples go through; however, they still have to be managed together as a couple. All these signs usually appear through that routine phase as a couple when you start becoming comfortable with each other's day-to-day lives, but something comes along and changes or breaks that routine. Many of these signs are also simply down to the fact that neither of you is putting effort into certain parts of the relationship that subsequently has a domino effect in other parts of your relationship.

SIGN 1: EFFORT IS BECOMING AN EFFORT

Earlier chapters discussed compromising for each other and putting in the work to strengthen the relationship. Though as you spend more time with your significant other, the effort may start dwindling for the simplest of things that kept the metaphorical spark of the relationship alive. You became comfortable with each other and that turned into a routine that requires little to no effort on the simple things such as going on dates or buying surprise gifts for each other. As a couple, it's easy to fall into this routine trap, and therefore becoming too comfortable with each other can become laziness. The act of doing things for each other outside of birthdays and special occasions becomes something that gets in the way when in the beginning it was something you may have gone out of your own way to do. However, there may be a limit to this as one individual in the couple may grow tired of this or it may affect them negatively. They may even try to put the effort into wanting to improve the relationship, but the other may be oblivious to the problem or simply be happy the way the relationship is.

People change over time, and you as an individual may struggle to admit it, but the right person can change the whole dynamic of another person's life for better or for worse. The idea of this sign is whether you can identify if your relationship is heading in this direction, or your relationship has already reached this point, of which you both should start doing the things that got you dating in the first place. That infatuation phase discussed earlier is where you can't wait to see the other person and constantly want to be with them. The myth of all this is that many couples believe that they can never get this phase back with each other, but in fact, it's very much possible to rekindle that energetic spirit between two people again. All it takes is an effort from both parties in a relationship and the willingness to retrace each other's steps as to how they started the relationship. The idea is to never give up on your relationship with someone if the cause cannot be justified to do so and you have exhausted all other possible options that lead you to this workbook.

SIGN 2: YOUR TIME IS SPENT ELSEWHERE

If you're a couple, especially one that may have been in a relationship for a very long time, the need to spend some time apart is just as important as spending time together. You want to still maintain your friendships and family relations while simultaneously maintaining a solid and strong relationship. Sometimes spending too much time with each other can cause agitation and boredom, so that time spent apart can give you that window period to miss each other again. However, if you start noticing that the two of you are excessively spending time apart from each other and becoming okay with that, it's an immediate red flag that you and your partner need to address immediately. It's important to establish that the best company is still with each other because even though you are in an intimate relationship, you are also each other's best friends. You should look at things you can do jointly as a couple, such as various destinations and activities you can do together, and also start taking a more concerted interest in each other's hobbies.

When you start taking interest in things that exclude your partner, it's often a difficult road to make a U-turn on. As emphasized before, relationships are a two-way street; it's important that this golden rule is followed and both parties come to the table. Another indicator for this can work. Often if one particular individual in a relationship is progressing, their attention may be on work and not the relationship. If you are experiencing this as the person working or the other way around, it's not something to be worried about initially. You want your partner to do well in his or her passions and goals, and it's your duty to help achieve it the best way with your know-how. However, there is a time and place for work, and it should not be something that revolves around the relationship. There are plenty of couples who encounter the scenario of choosing work or their relationship. It ultimately then comes down to what the two of you want to do regarding the work-life balance and just how bad it will affect your relationship.

SIGN 3: NO LONGER MAKING THE TIME

This is different from spending time elsewhere, but rather the time put aside to spend time with each other. In the early stages of a relationship, the couple will often go out of their way to see each other even if it means compromising other important plans. This naturally becomes less frequent in the later stages of a relationship because you tend to plan better and there is usually a better understanding of each other's time. However, problems arise when you or your partner have the time but choose not to make it available to each other. You will make excuses about how you may not have the time to do something and even the most mediocre issues take priority over the time you could have spent with your partner. This is something that every couple goes through at some point, and yes it is a normal occurrence, but should never be an increasing occurrence in a relationship.

No longer making time for each other can be argued as worse than spending your time elsewhere because here you may have all this free time to spend with your significant other, only to make an excuse not to spend it with them and even go as far as giving yourself more work. This then leads to the unfortunate fact that each other's company is no longer good for the both of you, though this does not mean the end of the relationship. When couples get stuck in the routine of doing the same things, they can become bored and therefore stop making time for each other—it's a reality that happens more commonly than most people think. The solution will then be for one of you to come up with something different that can test your comfort zone and provide interaction. The idea is to rekindle each other's company as the best company and motivate each other to explore different things that break the routine barrier. The boring routine that you can get to as a couple is the primary cause of this and is something that should always be tested and changed.

SIGN 4: THE SMALL THINGS STOP

The notion of "it's the small things that count," cannot resonate louder when it comes to the happiness and strength of a couple. Things such as cooking each other's favorite meals, surprise gifts, flowers, opening the door, and subtle touches that make you and your partner smile are what matter. The small things contribute to the overall bigger picture in a relationship and when these things start to fade away, relationships tend to start failing. It is essential to maintain those small things that put a smile on your partner's face because it's those things that they tend to remember the most, you just may not notice it. It gives your partner the indication that you are still trying and putting the effort into the relationship, and hopefully, that same effort is returned back. These small things don't necessarily have to be monetary things, they can stem from simple regular "I Love You" and a kiss on the forehead in the morning or goodnight messages when you are away from each other.

These are the things that often keep your relationship afloat and keep you together because, without these small significant things, there is no unique solid affection towards each other. These are things you often don't do with anyone else and are specifically for you and your partner. Other indicators can be the way you hold hands or a certain name you may have for each other. Once these things start changing it becomes an immediate red flag to you and your partner. The reason it becomes so noticeable is that it breaks the one positive routine between you and your partner, the one aspect of your relationship that should always remain a routine. It's these small fine lines or barriers that can often build up to something more serious that breaks a relationship down the line. It can, therefore, be argued that this sign is arguably the most important in terms of how quickly it can start negatively affecting your relationship. How a couple maintains their strength is unique to them through all the small efforts they put towards each other that cover the important parts of maintaining their relationship.

SIGN 5: ON DIFFERENT PAGES

Another factor that can cause problems for couples is when you start to disagree and not understand each other anymore. Now, this may sound confusing because when you are with someone in an intimate way, you should understand them as well as anyone close to them. However, couples can go through patchy periods of disagreement and misunderstanding. This is something normal that every couple goes through at some point in time. The fact of the matter is that your opinions will differ on certain things—some more serious than others—which will test the resolve of your relationship. The best way to go about handling this issue is by encouraging debate and opinion, creating conversation, and most importantly valuing each other's opinions regardless of the simplicity of the topic. Never ever disregard your partner's opinions, you both are equal members of the relationship and thus should be able to talk about anything.

However, there is a period in time when you or your partner starts deliberately disagreeing for no reason, and that's usually because of some other issue that is bothering one of you. Signals of this are usually through body language they project or the tone of voice that they use, though your partner or you should never disagree with each other without logical cause from both sides. Like in chapter one, communication is the key to understanding why you may be struggling to understand each other. No matter how long you have been in a relationship with someone, you are constantly learning new things about each other as you change together over time. Ask yourself the question, are you the same person you were at the beginning of the relationship to where you are now? These are the subtle small things that can deviate a couple from understanding each other. Try and put the joint effort in this period to turn your differences in opinion into something constructive through conversation and debate.

SIGN 6: LOOKING FOR CONFLICT

This is usually a sign when a couple starts getting frustrated with each other or seeks to take out their frustrations on one another because of some other external influence. As much as fighting is positive in a relationship if handled in the correct manner, there is no reason to seek conflict from your partner without genuine probable cause. This is both unfair to yourself and your partner and just serves to crumble the relationship from the inside out. By inside out, we refer to negatively affecting the emotions of each other until it eventually reflects physically. This is also a normal thing that couples go through usually because of factors such as friends, family, and work pressures, and often your partner becomes that person to unload all your emotions on. This is also not necessarily a bad thing as long as you don't direct the anger as if it's your partner's fault. If you are seeking conflict because of frustrations in your relationship, then you are going about dealing with it all wrong. You are pushing your partner away rather than encouraging them to have a talk about the problems in your relationship.

Often when couples become conflictive towards each other constantly, the relationship often struggles to rebound back to normal again. You may even see couples who are in a relationship with conflict all the time but never end up leaving each other usually out of fear of being alone. Again we turn to communication, but both of you need to come to a consensus on how you got into this conflictive period. Understand each other's reasoning and take the necessary measure to get your relationship back on the right track. Once again to help you with this, you can retrace your steps and go back to the best parts of your relationship. It's never a bad idea to be what you were in the early stages of your relationship, as many people might recall their best times in their relationships at the beginning. Unnecessary conflict can also come from when something breaks your routine with each other, and that change causes a problem rather than embracing that change together. When one part of your relationship is struggling, it's up to both of you to come together and make it a two-way street again.

SUMMARY

A couple consists of two people who need to put in the shared effort, otherwise, you will get certain problems that if not managed well or early enough, can easily have a detrimental effect on the relationship. These signs are typical and normal things that a couple will encounter throughout their relationship and should be seen as something couples can use to strengthen their relationship. It's important though to identify these signs when they start becoming more common and handle them as early as possible. Like with any problem, the earlier it is dealt with, the less damage can be done to all those involved. The first sign is an immediate red flag when one or both people in a relationship stop putting any effort in. This either means you stay together for the sake of it and routine or it will eventually boil over and possibly break the relationship beyond repair. If you ask any couple that has been together for many years, one of the key successes is that the effort never stopped, and when it did, they worked on it together. The next steps revolve around time and how you use the time as a couple. The problem comes when you are not spending time with each other by choice, but don't be confused with the time spent away from each other for reasons of work, friends, and family. However, if you are regularly neglecting to spend time with each other, this is a sign that you don't appreciate each other's company anymore. This is something that progresses longer into your relationship if you do not deal with it earlier.

Other signs are when you stop doing what the both of you did at the beginning of your relationship. These are the things that brought you into a relationship, to begin with, and should stay consistent throughout your time together. These small things often are often a pillar in the communication foundation that keeps your relationship strong. Simply ask yourself, are you doing the things that make your partner happy? The final signs then revolve around communication and conflict, which go hand in hand for all the reasons mentioned. It's never a good idea to get into any sort of conflict without a logical reason to back it up, and then to also handle it in a manner that is appropriate for all parties. If you find yourself in a relationship where you're turning tiny problems into big ones that is a sign of frustration from both sides either internally or externally in the relationship. There are many things in our day-to-day lives that can cause us frustration, and we sometimes need to take out the frustration on something or someone. Though always use your partner as a source of comfort for your frustrations your relationship should be built upon striving for each other's best selves.

Chapter 4
LET'S GET PHYSICAL

"There is a physical relationship that you have with a woman that you don't have with anybody else. But that's not about love. Love is a spiritual thing"
(Ziggy Marley Quote, n.d.).

The physical aspect of someone is what often attracts you as a person to another before you actually get to know them. In a relationship as you get more comfortable with each other, this becomes less relevant but is still healthy for you and your partner to maintain good physical contact. This does not just refer to activities behind closed doors but also simple acts such as holding hands, playing with each other, cuddling and any sort of positive physical contact you and your significant other tangibly share. This also plays a role in understanding your partner through body language without them having to say a word. Look at the people that are close around you, especially your parents. You can tell how they are feeling sometimes without even having to say a word. Physical contact also plays a role of being comfortable in each other's personal space; couples should never be afraid to let their partner into their personal space. Much like verbal communication, if there is no physical communication, a relationship will never last. There are occasions when your partner may want to be alone, it's then up to you to support their personal space and also understand the reasoning behind it either by reading their body language or simply verbalizing it to them.

However, this chapter will give you a step-by-step guide on how to rekindle that metaphorical physical fire in all parts of the relationship. The steps will also identify broad problems that may have caused issues in your relationship that lead to your relationship's current state. It's important to note that all these situations are normal problems couples go through, with all the physical changes and the comfort of not always needing physical contact as much as earlier in your relationship. Though, these are still steps in which you need to question yourself. Do any of these steps apply to you? Do you feel that your relationship lacks the necessary physical contact? Again, think about the reasons that you may or may not have this problem in your relationship, and see if any of the steps apply to you.

STEP 1: UNDERSTANDING EACH OTHER'S BODY LANGUAGE

To start, you change physically as a couple over time, so if you fall into this category, your perceptions and openness towards each other physically can indeed change drastically. So you may think you understand how to physically read your partner, but that can change overnight sometimes or even by the way you touch them. The bottom line is that your touch with your partner should always be a source of comfort and intimacy at all times. Many people communicate better with their body language and struggle to find the appropriate verbal manner to communicate—even as adults. You may think of yourself as a logical communicator, but that differs uniquely from person to person. Understanding your partner's physical cues also allows you to communicate with them using the right verbal manner. For example, they have had a frustrating day at work, you should then be their source of physical comfort, but misreading this can make the situation much worse.

Often couples who struggle to comfort each other physically have trust issues with one. The idea that you cannot be physically comfortable with someone you love automatically reduces attraction in all facets of the relationship. This is rare in longer relationships, though if you have this problem, the best way once again is to communicate it to your other half and put in the concerted effort to make it work. You can argue that it's more frustrating when someone cannot understand you physically than when they can't verbally. Remember, body language is the best way for a person to convey their true emotions about it, and therefore can be a true reflection of the strength of your relationship. Ask yourself, how do your relationship and your partner physically make you feel? Arguably the most important part of understanding your partner's body language is knowing when not to approach them, as the wrong timing in a physical confrontation can ruin a relationship quickly. That being said, most successful couples never have a reason to not approach each other, but personal space is something that should be respected.

STEP 2: A HEALTHY SEX LIFE

This is the most intimate form of physical interaction that a couple can have with each other. Though if you are a couple who is not married and have cultural reasons or something else to not have sex before marriage that is also perfectly fine as well. In this instance, you have both mutually agreed on this and therefore should not be a problem in your relationship until after marriage—however, this step still applies to you for when you get to that stage. This is often a very sensitive topic for couples to talk about but is a necessary part of a healthy relationship. The act itself is in your most vulnerable state and should always stay between you and your partner. However, as couples grow older, that physical lust of the younger days can dwindle. This is common amongst older couples, but if you are a young couple with this problem, it's a much more serious worry. The first and most obvious problem is physical changes that cause less attraction, but this is part of life and you have to accept that you and your partner will grow old. A good way, however, to get around this is by "spicing" things up in the bedroom so to speak. The fact is that couples may stick to the same sexual routine eventually makes them become bored with each other. Change it up and try different things behind closed doors to get that adrenaline rush back as if it was the first time. Do things out of your comfort zone but be sure not to hurt yourself. You don't want a bedroom malfunction or something sensitive to stop working if you get what I mean.

Sex proves to your partner that you are attracted to them. Changing it up shows your partner that you are still attracted to them more than ever. Never have sex for the sake of having sex with your partner. It is a sacred act that both of you need to be fully committed to, which many people do not realize. Be honest and ask yourself are you enjoying sex with your partner? If you are a young couple and this is an issue, change it up as well. The only way to make it better is to do things differently. With all this being said, it's important that these urges are managed well with your partner. Everyone has different sexual needs and urges, and you may be with someone that is very conservative. If this is the case, give them time to get comfortable; if you are trying something new, make sure they are comfortable. The fact is you can get so caught up in the act and need to maintain a healthy sex life but forget how to make it an activity the both of you enjoy.

STEP 3: HAVE JOINT BODY GOALS

There has never been a time in human history when people have focused as much on their bodies as they do today. You see many couples who have a joint goal of having desired bodies. What this does is build that physical attraction towards each other, but it also makes you both comfortable when you are working together for that desired physique. You become each other's motivators, and this will serve your relationship positively. This also gives you the time to recommend to your partner where they can physically improve without offending them too much. The reality is that many relationships end when one individual in the relationship stops caring about their physical self. This in turn makes your partner less physically attracted to you. Positive physical change can do wonders for not only the confidence of the individual but the confidence of a couple in general. When you feel you look better, this increases confidence and therefore spills off into all other parts of your relationship.

When it comes to things that relate to one's self-image in a relationship, it's always best to do things together. Remember that your partner is your pillar of comfort, strength, and motivation. Use this and feed off each other; this is not only building that positive self-image together but team-building each other as a couple and building trust to solve all your other problems. You may be a couple for years and still not have that element of full trust with one another but doing something like this narrows that gap. This also translates to all those people that are close to you, and this just further strengthens the relationship. There is no feeling like getting compliments from other couples or people about how well you are doing as a couple. Having and achieving joint goals, in general, is a good way to feed off each other's positive energy.

STEP 4: THE COMFORT AND HAPPINESS OF TOUCH

This refers to all the physical contact outside of sex, all those small touches and cues that give two people in the relationship comfort and happiness. The act of simply holding hands as a couple is an underrated method of strengthening the bond between two people. You might be a couple that has a healthy sex life but lacks the fundamentals of just kissing each other or even cuddling together. Physical contact in a relationship is not strictly about sex, because there are couples out there who don't need sex to have a fantastic relationship. The simplest touch of letting someone know you are there or putting your arms around them can change their mood a full 360 degrees. We see it not just in relationships, but in how we interact with friends, or even in the sports environment. Do you not feel awkward if you do not hug or shake your best friend's hand when you meet them? It's a biological need in all humans to touch, and when that process is initiated, it's the first sign of small trust you place in someone. When last as a couple did you cuddle and watch a movie together? When last did you just sit in each other's arms and talk about anything?

This can relate to maintaining the simple acts in a relationship that forms part of the bigger picture. These small physical cues and acts carry a lot of weight when maintaining the happiness, strength, and comfort of a relationship. A golden rule to remember is that these small acts are free to your partner, so there should be no reason why they should not be a staple part of the relationship. These touches are one of the first things to disappear when a couple is going through tough times or problems, and therefore is a solid indicator that your relationship may require some intervention to get it back to normal again in the near future.

STEP 5: IT'S OKAY TO HAVE BOUNDARIES

As much as embracing physical contact with your partner is positive, there is no issue with having boundaries to your personal space every once in a while. This kind of situation is uncommon, but usually applies to couples who are more conservative than others, so it can be seen as a unique situation. Sometimes it's a good idea to be away from each other's physical presence, even in the same household. It sometimes strengthens a couple by appreciating that they have each other. The act of missing one's physical presence in a relationship is healthy for a couple. It increases physical attraction and also gives you time to think about things outside the relationship itself. The problems arise when the alone time you spend away from your partner becomes something more enjoyable, which can be narrowed down to problems of not getting along with each other. Therefore, don't forget that you set boundaries as a couple for personal reflection and much-needed alone time, but if you don't eventually miss your partner's company, you have time to reflect on ways to change that. Why don't you miss them? Are you the one that is the problem? Are you not putting in the effort and vice versa? Ultimately, voluntarily spending time away from each other should not be the norm.

The primary goal though of setting these boundaries is knowing and appreciating you have someone outside of friends and family that you have to go back to. It can further strengthen your relationship as you reflect on why you are with that person and if you love them.

STEP 6: MAINTAIN STEPS 1 TO 5

The premise of these steps is that you can use them all together in the order they are set out. To start off, you need to understand your partner before you can move on to the next step. You need to understand how they interact with themselves, yourself, and others in a physical manner. Identify those physical social cues, so you can act accordingly when they need that physical contact. Take it upon yourself to ensure they know you are a source of safety, comfort, strength, and motivation no matter the situation. Most importantly, work on it together so that you can maximize your understanding of each other, especially if you misunderstand each other from time to time. Once you understand the basic physical and personality traits of your partner, bedroom talk becomes a lot easier and you can move towards understanding each other from a sexual perspective. There is not a lot that can be said here because it's unique to the two people in the relationship, and sex differs from couple to couple, so it's up to you as a couple to find that equilibrium. As your relationship grows in strength through days, weeks, months, and years, so does the physical attraction towards each other. It's important that your physical feelings towards each other do nothing but only get better over time using points provided for the bedroom and having goals. Embracing each other's physical features whether through sex or through simple touch is something that keeps that physical attraction alive.

You need to maintain all those small physical interactions that are unique to both of you. The more unique it is, the better it is because it's something of high personal value and affection towards one another. An example of this would be having pet names for each other, having a certain way of kissing each other or having a way or ritual of holding hands. These need to be maintained and you will find your relationship thriving that much more in the long term. Now that you have reached this period of near-perfect physical contact with each other, try not to make it too overbearing for each other. Take that necessary alone time period because, at some point or time for all couples, one or the other is going to want some time alone or away not necessarily because there is a problem in the relationship. The idea is then to miss one another and the company of having someone you can be intimate with. Lastly, maintain this throughout the relationship and repeat it where it's needed.

SUMMARY

This chapter seeks to improve the physical aspect of the relationship for a couple and how you can achieve that. Physical contact in a relationship is just as important as the verbal part. The steps in this chapter are ones that you will repeat throughout the life cycle of your relationship in some shape or form outside these steps. The steps are just a solid guideline to follow to accurately improve the physical aspects of your relationship. Starting with understanding your partner and their physical personality traits is the foundation of this chapter. If you don't understand your partner, you will not know where to start. So once you start embracing each other and your physical differences you can start moving towards the more sensitive step of your relationship. The idea of talking about working through a couple's sex life is a difficult thing. It's a topic that most people don't really like to talk about but it's necessary for a healthy relationship. Basically, embrace it and work on the betterment of your sex life through the point provided.

We then move to set up goals, which regardless of whether it's personal or between multiple people is something generally healthy to have. As a couple working towards something meaningful—even if you don't quite achieve it—builds the bond and strength of a couple. Having goals together helps with so many aspects of the relationship such as motivation and being there for each other. This step tells that this should be something mandatory to have for not only the physical aspects but for other aspects you may both be struggling in. You then learn about the aspects and positivity of just simply touching each other outside the realms of the bedroom; arguably this can be seen as more important than the sexual aspect of the relationship. This is a step that must be consistently maintained as related to the final step. Then establishing positive boundaries for one another, will be the sole goal of missing each other to strengthen that bond and need to be with one another. This is something that does not necessarily have to be done often, but it's a good idea to have some alone time to reflect on other things and know you have a cushion—someone—to go back to in an intimate sense. Lastly, the primary goal of maintaining all these steps is to make sure you maximize the results should this be an issue in your relationship. It's important to note that couple problems are always best dealt with together.

58 *Are you enjoying this book? If so, I'd be really happy if you could leave a short review on Amazon. It means a lot to me! Thank you.*

Chapter 5
MENTAL STIMULATION

"Love looks not with the eyes, but with the mind, and therefore is winged Cupid painted blind" (A Midsummer Night's Dream, n.d.).

You have gone through the steps needed to improve the physical aspect of your relationship, now the idea of this chapter is the mental aspect of a couple. Mental health regardless of relationships is important for yourself as a human being; however, in a relationship, it works a bit differently than just health. The focus is on how you stimulate each other as a couple outside the physical aspects of your relationship. Now that you have the tools for the physical aspect, you need to tackle verbal, written, and communicative stimulation between the two of you. The ability to talk to each other about anything and everything in a relationship is essential to a happy life together. This chapter will guide you to the mental stimulants you can use to help you with this aspect as a couple. Though before that can be learned, it's important to understand what is meant by mental stimulation in a relationship.

WHAT IS THE PURPOSE OF MENTAL STIMULATION

Mental stimulation in a relationship is not as complicated as it sounds; it refers to not only the communication between couples but if that communication is relevant to them. For example, you may share a common interest in something of discussion or relevance. Whatever this interest is, you use it to speak to each other for the purposes of enriching the mind. Mental stimulation is not to be confused with communication, because the focus is on stimulating the mind on topics that bring a couple together they discuss. Another example is the common interests that got you and your partner into a relationship. You shared common interests that created good conversation which sparked the mental attraction either before or after the physical attraction. Unlike physical attraction, a person's mind remains the same as long as they are alive, and as a couple being able to mentally stimulate each other is something that can bypass physicality. Some people are attracted by the looks of their partner and others are attracted by their partner's ability to stimulate their mind positively.

Another purpose of mental stimulation is to help a couple understand things as one. You start thinking alike or understand what your partner is thinking through your shared interests in debate and conversation. This also makes communication between couples—especially in the early stages—easier because you have common ground with each other. If the physical attraction does not bring a couple closer, often the mental aspect can save the relationship because this is usually something unique you have with your partner. If you have been in multiple relationships, it's highly unlikely it would have been the exact same as your others because everyone is different. Looks are temporary but the mind is forever in this case. So how can you maintain or encourage mental stimulation in a relationship?

FIND YOUR COMMON INTERESTS

Every person is unique in their own way, but when it comes to a relationship there are certain similarities that brought you together in the first place. These are usually topics of interest you like talking about, which brings about happiness for the two of you. This is unique to every relationship, so it's up to you as a couple to find those common interests. The mental stimulus comes from the enjoyment of doing something you both love. This can be as simple as taking a walk together, having debates on your favorite topics, going to your favorite date spot, and so on. These are usually things you did together often at the beginning of your relationship that you don't do as much now. This, in turn, is where the problem of boredom in a relationship can arise because you no longer share any common interests with each other. It's also possible that you discourage each other to the point where these interests are no longer interests anymore. Never ruin the things in your relationship that you can share, as there are often not many things without having to compromise.

For example, you may see couples who are total opposites in a really good relationship and it's not because opposites attract. The reason is often that there are one or few things that they really like doing together and they focus on those aspects to keep their relationship going in the long run. As said before the physical characteristics of a person will change but subconsciously it's the mental aspect of each other that keeps it together. The best examples are elderly couples. They are still attracted to each other because they still find ways to interact with each other outside the physical realm. When you find that common interest with your partner, hold onto it and never let it go because it can be the thing that saves your relationship in the future. You may not notice it now, but after reading this, pay attention to what happens if you don't interact with each other's shared interests; you would almost get an immediate negative response or demeanor from your partner.

Find Shared Interests in Differences

As a backup plan, it's always a good idea to take an interest in mental stimulants that interest your partner. For example, you may be an individual who loves a particular sport, but on the other hand, your partner hates it. The idea is to find common ground and stimulus that you can relate to when watching the sport. This can be things such as educating your partner on the rules of the sport to help them understand the basics of it. On some occasions, they may take a concerted interest in it with you because of the effort you went through to share your interests and passions. Mental stimulation comes from the joy of being able to share something you once did on your own or with other people, with the person you are in a relationship with. Think about something you love doing that your partner is not necessarily interested in. Then imagine them interacting with you in interest or passion. That image alone has already stimulated you in a positive way without it actually happening. Now if that imagination becomes a reality that is a huge win for your relationship. However, as discussed before, this is a two-way effort, and your partner must take an active interest to want to do this with you.

On the other hand, you may be in a relationship because of the differences you have, in which it's then important to understand whether your partner wants to share their passions and interests with you. For example, your partner might do painting as a mental getaway from the world. What can happen is that's their personal space that they don't wish to share for good reason usually. However, there is no harm in taking interest because it can be something that makes good "dinner conversation," thus you may not quite be taking part in the painting together, but you found commonality nonetheless through conversation. By now this should give you a good idea of what to focus on regarding your partner, especially if you have no shared common interests. In that case, it then can be referred to as opposites attract because the differences between you two are what makes you attracted to each other. They may seem obvious, but couples tend to be oblivious to these kinds of things until there are problems in the relationship.

MENTAL STIMULATION IS GOOD FOR YOUR HEALTH

Lastly, mental stimulation is good for your health in the sense that you don't require a medical professional to help you with it. Positive mental stimulation using the above difference and interests is a catalyst for happiness in a relationship. A happy couple is a stable and strong relationship that works together in maintaining the relationship as it is. Fortunately, when you get this aspect of your relationship right, it becomes infectious because it does rely on the physical realm. However, you cannot spend time together as a couple without being able to mentally stimulate each other because this would create an awkward situation. Yet this is something that happens in couples after they feel they have nothing to talk about. Again, never get caught up in that routine of doing the same things all the time as a couple. You can keep the routine to a certain point but change it up a little.

The most important aspect of your health is that mental stimulation prevents depression and boredom in a couple. It may not seem easy, but depression can happen even in a relationship. This is usually when one half of your couple puts in the effort to share interests and passions with each other but is immediately rejected by the other, more often than not without even realizing it. Thus, you or your partner can become depressed from actual neglect. So mental stimulation can really be something that can genuinely save your relationship. Though what specific common issues can it solve?

What Couple Problems Does It Solve

The common times you would ever need to use mental stimulation to help your relationship is when your relationship becomes stale and you take less interest in each other because of the daily routine once again. We then refer to "effort" by both parties in attempting to find something to rekindle interest back with one another. Another reason to use mental stimulation is that when you feel physical attraction debilitating, it's a good alternative. This mainly applies to how you view yourself physically. If you are having self-doubts about your appearance, you can always revert to what you're good at with your partner. It's also important to note that if a person is with you for your looks, it will never last in the long term. Remember, looks are temporary and the mind is permanent. You want the person you are with to like or love you for your mind first and foremost.

SUMMARY

This chapter covers something in more detail that many couples' intimacy books do not cover in as much detail. Mental stimulation is indeed the constant in a relationship when the physical aspect of your relationship starts declining. The mental aspect is what keeps your couple going strong, and you are able to maintain happiness as a unit. The importance of mental stimulation cannot be stressed enough, as it's not only good for the happiness of your relationship but also for the health of both of you in the relationship. Discuss what the best ways are to properly use mental stimulus in your relationship. This revolves around either using your interests or differences in the best way possible with your partner and vice versa. The final product of this is to increase the happiness and compatibility between each other in your relationship for the importance of staying together for the long term. Mental stimulation does not age like the physical aspect of a relationship and therefore can definitely be seen as an alternative and fail-safe.

We then discuss its relation to health and how it can pull someone out of depression. Happiness is good for the health of an individual and for a relationship as a whole. Sharing interests and differences with one another is up there with the most rewarding experiences as a couple. It strengthens the bond and may even bring the "I love you" out if it has not been said already. Use it to break the couple's routines that have created boredom or depression. Put in the effort and do things together to stimulate each other's minds. As with everything in bettering a relationship, the most effective results will come from the mutual effort needed from both sides of the party in your relationship and is no different when it comes to mental stimulation. Once you find that consensus and equilibrium, hold on to it and never let it go because your relationship may depend on it in the present and future.

Chapter 6
CONFLICT AND TRUST RESOLUTION

"The greater your capacity to love, your greater capacity to feel pain" **(Jennifer Aniston Quotes, n.d.).**

Conflict is part and parcel of a relationship. It's an inevitable problem then every single couple goes through. How you deal with conflict can define all aspects of your relationship for a day, a week, or a month, or completely ruin the relationship. As much as conflict is good for a relationship, there is a fine line where it can become too much for a couple. Verbal conflict as discussed earlier is something normal and can be worked on, but as soon as it becomes physical, it can be very difficult to rebuild a relationship. The reason it is difficult is that it directly affects the trust in a relationship. Trust is something that takes a while to build up for most people; it's something that is truly earned, but once it's betrayed it can take a very long time to get back. However, there are ways to address the issues of conflict and trust using various steps and communication.

CONFLICT RESOLUTION STEPS

These are the common steps you can use for various scenarios when you are having issues of conflict in your relationship. It's important to understand that how you resolve the conflict between one another can define the trajectory of your relationship as a couple. After, focus on the steps that relate to you the most out of the current problems you are having as a couple and apply them accordingly. These steps may seem obvious, but then you would not be seeking the help of a couple's intimacy workbook, and there would be no conflict in your relationship. Unlike children, as adults, we tend not to focus on the obvious and overthink everything.

Conflict is something that's very broad. These steps will not help you if the conflict is something very serious that warrants the betrayal of trust and the end of the relationship. For example, if you are caught having an affair, that is something that simple steps cannot solve because you have placed your feelings with another individual. It's always wise to think about the severity of the conflict. Have you done something that warrants an immediate break-up or divorce? Is it something that may take months or even years to get back? Did you do it because you no longer want to be with your current partner? These are serious questions one needs to ask themselves before even dealing with the actual problem of conflict.

Step 1: Always Be Honest

It's important that you don't lie to your partner to solve your problem. This is immediately betraying their trust, something which you may have worked extremely hard for. Tell them the problem as it is, be honest about it, and don't leave any important details out when resolving a conflict. Doing this makes it easier for your partner to understand your version of events and also makes them comfortable enough not to lie back to you. In relationships, once one lies to the other, the lies then start becoming something both individuals participate in because trust has been abandoned. There is absolutely nothing wrong with being honest and avoiding the truth to not offend your partner is wrong for both of you. You need to be able to openly talk about anything no matter how shameful it may be because we are all human and we make mistakes. Always understand that no one is perfect, and as a couple problems will be easier to tackle and identify without blowing over unnecessarily.

If your conflict is severe enough to break up your relationship, the best answer is still to be honest about it. Your partner may value honesty enough to continue the relationship with you, but this will differ from person to person. Honesty is indeed the best policy in a relationship.

Step 2: Listen

In a relationship, both individuals' opinions should matter equally; there is no room for dominance over the opinions of the other. Value the opinions of your partner in a conflict and listen to the reasons they provide because you may very well be the one in the wrong. If you don't listen to your other half in a relationship, there is no point in communicating, to begin with, it becomes an irrelevant and pointless act. When both of you listen to each other's honest opinions in a conflict, the solutions come quicker, and the trust grows stronger. Listening especially in situations of conflict allows you to learn and understand your partner better, so it can be dealt with better in the future. When your partner feels valued in the relationship, you are already preventing a plethora of problems that you may encounter in the future. As always, make sure both parties have equal time to listen and explain their side of a conflict.

Step 3: Be Patient

Sometimes a conflict can be resolved but it takes a while for people to calm down or accept it and move on. It's also best to give your partner as much time as possible to calm down or give them time to think. You are respecting your partner's personal space by doing this and that time waiting made it easier for the both of you to communicate. Everyone is different, and therefore acts and responds to conflict differently there is no exact category or science that everyone falls into. Some just need more time than others, especially if it's something personal or means a lot to them. Being patient is also a positive trait to have. Your partner will understand that you will never rush them into anything uncomfortable. All this does is further build and solidify the trust and respect between two people. Even in the worst situations, the time you give your partner to think about it means they will make a decision that is not rash or impulsive.

Step 4: Always Offer Support

Even if you are having a spur-of-the-moment hatred toward each other, it's still important to show support in the conflict. You want your partner to trust you in the future when it comes to things that cause conflict outside the relationship because you have your own lives at the end of the day. By still showing support through conflict, it signifies that no matter how bad things get, you will still love each other at the end of the day. This also turns a conflictive situation into something healthy. Ask any couple in a relationship for a significant amount of time. They will support each other even in situations when they do not want to because that is just part of being in a loving relationship with someone.

Step 5: Keep Conflict Between Each Other

We often ask friends and family for advice in times of crisis and conflict. However, in a relationship, it's always best to keep it with the people involved in the conflict. If you are fighting with each other, keep it between each other. The only time you go to family and friends for advice is when the situation becomes something bordering abuse. Then it's recommended to let someone know that your partner is abusing you and your safety has been compromised. If it's just a simple but serious fight, then try not to tell anyone else about it and as covered before, do not make it open to the public. If you trust each other in a relationship, then you trust that you will find the solution to problems you encounter together. If you are having conflict outside your relationship with other people, that is unfortunately out of your control, but stick together and support each other as a couple, no matter what.

TRUST RESOLUTION

Trust is truly something that is earned and is probably the hardest thing to earn from a person. Everyone is different and takes longer than some to place their trust in someone. Trust is also something that can instantly be lost, even with all the effort gone into obtaining it. You see, when someone places their trust in you, it can be described as a turtle leaving its shell; you are sharing your vulnerability with someone else. So, if the problem in your relationship is trust, then there are steps you can use to earn it or earn it back. This is one of the few things in a relationship where one individual controls all the power. When you betray the trust of your partner, they dictate the timeline as to when you can get it back and you will have no other option but to wait.

Step 1: Take Your Time

If you are trying to earn the trust of your partner, make sure to not rush them or put them in uncomfortable situations to force it. On the other hand, if you are the person waiting for the time to place your trust, make sure you think long and hard about it. Understand that trust is a big deal in a relationship because it opens up all those personal doors to someone. Once again, understanding your partner comes into play, and make sure to value their trust as if it were the last drop of water in the world. Take your time in earning trust with your partner and wait for the right time to be sure about placing trust in your partner.

Step 2: Earn Trust

If you are in that stage in your relationship where you are looking to earn the trust of each other for certain things, always make sure you act in a manner that does not make your partner think otherwise. There may be small habits about you that are preventing this for whatever reason but try your best to prove to your partner that you are trying without the need to tell them. Always refer back to what placing trust in someone means and also look at where the valued trust is for you, such as where does trust fall in terms of importance in your life? On the other hand, if you are looking to earn your trust back, this is a trickier situation because it's entirely unique to every individual. Your partner might be someone who values trust above all else, and in this case, you may have to gradually earn it over time again. On the positive side, if you are in a relationship after either one of you somehow betrayed one another's trust in some way, this means you are willing to give your partner time to earn it back.

This is when stepping one aids step two, and it becomes a waiting game that does not have a concrete timeline. Understand what your partner is going through and respect them enough to earn it back. If you are on the rare occasion where you are in a relationship with someone you don't trust wholeheartedly, your relationship will not progress to any sort of fruition.

Step 3: Don't Force It

The worst thing you can do with regard to trust is force someone into a situation to test it. As a couple there will be situations out of your control where your trust and bond are tested; there is no need to bring up situations to try and force it out of your partner. Wait for the situations to naturally come. It has to be something out of your control, otherwise, how can you tell if it's genuine trust? Moreover, you create an uncomfortable situation and it sends the wrong message to your partner—in some cases making you less trustworthy.

Step 4: Do Things Together

One of the quickest and best ways to earn trust or earn it back in a relationship is by doing things together as a couple. In this way, you are more likely to encounter situations that will test the trust of your relationship. Don't ever look at situations whether conflictive or trust testing as a bad thing. It's just another opportunity to test how strong the foundations of your relationship are as well as reinforce those foundations even more. The basis of a couple is the ability to do things together, otherwise, why are you together? Though understand that doing things together is not solely about earning the trust of your partner. If you are doing it for this reason, then you are doing it wrong. There are couples out there who do things together for reassurance that they are still attracted to each other, and this is not healthy for the relationship. Always be in the moment with each other and not think about achieving objectives with each other when together. It's always best to let things happen naturally, which is a key success to a good relationship.

COMBINE CONFLICT AND TRUST STEPS

Conflict and trust go hand in hand and depending on how much you trust someone can often determine the outcome of a conflictive situation. Therefore, combining the steps for trust and conflict is the perfect way to tackle the serious conflictive situation that will make or break the trust in a relationship. Honesty plays a role in both conflict and trust and is one of the primary catalysts for trust in a relationship. If you view someone as an honest person, more often than not you are willing to place your trust in that person. The idea of these steps is to cater to the unique situation you find yourself in and combine the steps that apply to you. You could be in a situation where you are trying to earn trust or trying to earn back for one of your wrongdoings. However, you should not confuse the two. When you are trying to earn someone's trust, it's much easier because you are both starting from a clean slate; there is nothing for you to make you think otherwise. When you cause a situation that causes someone not to trust you anymore or for at least that time being, this will be a difficult uphill battle.

The key component of both conflict and trust is the combination of patience and time. These two particular steps will always have a place in any situation. Therefore, both steps are a good starting point to use, and then you apply other steps that relate to your particular situation. The idea of bettering your resolution skills is to try your best to solve the problems that are in your personal and particular situation. If you or your partner cannot relate to the steps provided, it will never work. That's why for this particular chapter, you are given options that you can use to cater for not just conflict and trust, but other avenues you see fit.

SUMMARY

The basic premise of this chapter is to give you the flexibility in solving those conflicts and trust problems. Often, people read steps and feel the need to follow them in that particular order for maximum success. Though everything may not necessarily apply to your situation and you may find yourself involved in pointless acts that don't help you. Therefore, it's important you understand the defining components of what is conflict and trust, and what you need to look for and develop the best plan to address them. Resolving conflict is not purely based on following everything you are told or read about; it's about following the applicable points that you feel mean something to you. If you look at the steps of conflict, there will always be at least more than one step applied to you because patience will always apply in any form of conflict in your relationship. If you summarize conflict as a whole, the need for time and patience will become prevalent at some point in time. Patience is a good trait to have because it prevents you from making irrational decisions and thinking through decisions carefully. Combine this with honesty and you are well on your way to earning trust and solving the conflict sooner. As covered before, there should only ever be honesty in relationships no matter how bad the truth is.

Trust is always something that is earned. You cannot buy someone's trust; it's a social value system that everyone has without a price. Trust between couples makes them both vulnerable to pain and it's a sensitive line that can be cut in a second if handled the wrong way. Since trust can't be bought, it most definitely can't be forced, just like how you can't force someone to like you no matter how much effort you may put into them. Fortunately, because you are a couple, this is not something you have to worry about as long as you are open and honest with your partner and you are there for them when they need you, even if you are going through a period of trust and conflict with them. The reward for conquering and pushing through it together is a unique feeling that only strong couples will know. It's one of the greatest feelings as a couple breaking boundaries together and just simply growing with the right person. The feeling is almost as if life could not get any better, so keep that in mind as a motivating factor for both of you when going through tough times.

Chapter 7
APPRECIATE THE DIFFERENCES

"Don't settle for a relationship that won't let you be yourself" **(Oprah Winfrey Quotes, n.d.)**

Couples often believe that it's the similarities between each other that make the relationship work. Some people even wonder if they could date themselves because there would be no problems. However, it's virtually impossible to find someone who shares the same interests and traits as you. Even identical twins have differences about them as they get older and develop their own personalities. If you had to logically think about if you had to date someone who was identical to you in all facets of life, there would be a point where that becomes boring and even frustrating because that lack of difference doesn't make the relationship unique or exciting. Chances are that you are a couple who have commonly shared differences, or you are a couple that embraces the fact that you are different in every way. At the end of the day, you should be in a relationship with someone for who they are as a person and nothing else to be successful as possible.

Appreciating the differences in each other is also one of the most rewarding experiences and creates well comradely in a relationship. There are always insecurities that you and your partner bring into a relationship because you are different people; your roles are then to make those insecurities something you can openly share with each other. Never place the blame or make fun of your partner for their differences even if it's a light-hearted moment. Make sure that when you are joking about something concerning your partner, it's not something that is deeply personal to them. Many problems are caused by being different people in a relationship. This once again is not a bad thing and can be seen as a constructive opportunity to appreciate the things that are different about each other. Though there are some problems that need to be addressed when you are trying to work around each other's differences in a certain manner.

DIFFERENCE OF OPINION

Probably the biggest cause of verbal disagreements between couples can be quite serious if the both of you are two very strong opinionated people. This can often make the simplest problems into the biggest issues just because you refused to accept and respect the opinions of one another. You will never ever agree on everything as a couple. There are too many things in the world, and there will come a time when you have an argument about them. The difference of opinion in a relationship is a good thing though and should turn from a problem to something constructive. A difference of opinion shows you have your own strong set of values and not some kind of person who follows whatever anyone says. Arguments are healthy in a relationship as long as you have mutual respect for each other.

If you have a different opinion on something in a relationship, refrain from keeping it to yourself even if it might not be to your partner's liking. We can all view the same situation differently; therefore, sometimes an honest second opinion is not the worst to look at something differently. Lastly, the difference of opinion stimulates thinking for couples and asks them to not only question themselves, but the person they are with as well. In a disagreement with your partner, always accept the fact that you might be the one in the wrong, as it can be a good humbling experience for the both of you.

DIFFERENCE IN PERSONALITY

Apart from opinions, the people you are in a relationship with are also different. More often than not couples are with each other because for the most part, their personalities work well together. There are also couples who like certain aspects of each other but compromise their personality to be with each other, but this is not necessarily the right way to be with someone. This comes back to understanding who you are with and what makes them tick. Personalities can also change in a relationship, sometimes for the better or for worse depending on the issues you are going through. Either of you can change to match each other better or change when tough times require you to be a certain way. There are times in your relationship when problems are caused by one of you acting out of character, and this is perfectly normal. The ideal solution as usual would be just to sit with one another and talk about it. Always remember, you should be with someone for who they are and nothing else.

Another part of this is when one part of the couple tries to change the personality of the other or make them think differently. However, you may succeed by changing a few things, but ultimately a person's values and ethics never change once it's established. It's also greedy of an individual to try and manipulate someone for their own personal preference, especially when it comes to someone you are intimate with. There are certain things that you may want to change or need to change for your partner. If these changes are only in the best interest of the relationship, then it's more than welcome to go through the process of it. This often happens when couples decide to live together, and certain things need to be changed to live compatible. When you start trying to enforce big changes on the person you are with that was never an issue before, this is where unnecessary problems can occur. However, you can voice your opinion so that they are aware of it.

INSECURITIES

Often as couples, we bring insecurities into the relationship with us, and these are often sensitive and take time to open up about them. These insecurities can have a direct effect on a couple's sex life and even physical contact in general, but it's usually for a reason that's worthy of it. The idea is to work on these insecurities together if possible or give your partner time to open up about them. These insecurities are often things that relate to the physical and/or are usually matters where a person feels like they are the only ones in the world with that problem. Insecurities can often cause couples to fight without even having an existing cause for the fight; it's just something that triggered it when you were together. It's often best to just communicate about it and come up with an action plan of how you are going to do it. It's important to respect the wishes of your partner because these matters are often sensitive.

The reward from all this is when your partner finally opens up about it. To reiterate, it's again a feeling unique to someone you have an intimate connection with. It instantly strengthens the bond between two people and allows a person to really show their vulnerable side. If you are the one that's insecure in the relationship, try not to keep it bottled up for too long unless you are fully in control. For example, you may be insecure about something on your body. The reality is that when you eventually become more sexual with your partner, you will have to make them aware of it and they should ensure you that they will do their best to make you as comfortable as possible. In this type of scenario, if you are with the right person, they will respect it and not brush it off as something small. Problems are caused when from your point of view, your partner's insecurities seem silly, but remember that everyone views the same thing differently, so don't come across as arrogant and dominant.

Always remember that insecurities are unique and different for your partner than what they may be for you. They can be both physical and emotional, and as a collective in a relationship, you need to understand your partner's insecurities when they choose to share them with you. Never ever discourage your partner about their insecurities and always motivate them to either deal with or overcome such insecurities, make sure they know you are there for the support they should need. Sometimes just knowing someone is there for you is enough for you to conquer your insecurities alone.

LIFE AND CULTURAL DIFFERENCES

In the modern world of dating, we are seeing more interracial couples every year. Often these ethnic and cultural differences always make the individuals in a relationship feel like they are involved in something different all the time and that is indeed beautiful. However, you can fall in love with a person but not necessarily their background or cultural choice that can put both of you in some uncomfortable situations. You can also be someone from an underprivileged background dating someone from a wealthy family. We see these things so much in movies and the difficulty that couples go through in trying to combat the external influences that affect their relationship negatively. Though you will only ever understand the full scale of it once you are in a relationship together. Life and cultural differences often involve family members and friends, which brings a whole lot of other problems sometimes. This is particularly awkward if you are an interracial couple, a same-sex couple, if you are wealthy or not, if you practice a religion or if you don't believe in religion at all.

The harsh reality is that you will be judged by other people in your partner's circle for your differences on occasions, but as long as you have the support of your partner, that's really all that matters. If we combine religion together, one of these four factors will at some point be an uncomfortable point of conversation when interacting with each other's families. If you are ever at a point where you are feeling uncomfortable around the people your partner calls friends or family, be sure to let them know about it, but as usual, keep it between the two of you. Thus, your partner knows what to look out for when you are uncomfortable around other people in your life and stays by your side when you need it. Couples are often oblivious to these kinds of things because their partner may feel awkward telling them about a bad experience with family and friends. Many people choose to believe that their friends and family act a certain way, and it can be difficult to learn that this may not always be the case.

SUMMARY

This chapter is about embracing the differences of each other and how to deal with those differences when they become difficulties in a relationship. Throughout this book, you are constantly reminded that you should be with someone for who they are and nothing else. The reason is to remind you as the reader why you and your partner are or will be going through the effort of fixing your relationship in the present or future. Turning your differences and personality into something constructive is the basics of dealing with each other's differences. At the beginning of relationships, people try to find common ground that keeps them coming back to each other and creates mental and physical attraction. You find the differences in each other as your relationship progresses to a more comfortable state and that can be overwhelming sometimes. The purpose of all this is being different and embracing each other's different opinions, values, and traits and these are what make a relationship all the more unique.

Further discussed is dealing with the sensitive topic of insecurities, the one thing that the individuals in relationships take time to build towards sharing with each other. Insecurities are different among all people, but some are more similar than others. You may be insecure about something that your partner is very confident about, and they may struggle to get to grips with that. When you are really good at something and others are struggling, you may struggle to appreciate or understand their difficulty, which is the same for insecurities. So give your other half time to deal with their demons that you may not see as a big deal.

It shows you value and respect them in a manner you can only imagine when the attitude is returned back to you. Lastly, we touched upon the small matter of life and cultural differences, which are incredibly tricky to work around when you're dealing with new people who you hope to see you in a certain way. It's scary as a couple when you come from very different backgrounds and families trying to keep a relationship stable when things go wrong. Always support each other, even if those around you don't. It can be a very lonely place in a relationship for a couple when one does not feel supported.

Chapter 8
NEVER COMPARE AND ACCEPTING THE WRONG

"It was a million tiny little things that, when you added them all up, they meant we were supposed to be together… and I knew it" **(Yasharoff, 2018).**

Couples tend to start comparing themselves to others when things go wrong. They may even want to be like other couples they know or even follow on television and social media. The idea is to achieve the happiness and strength of successful couples and emulate that as close as possible to your relationship. The problem comes when you start wanting to be a couple and people you are not; this never works when you are in a relationship for the reasons of being who you are. Just because you are going through rough times as a couple, does not mean you have to change yourself or yourselves as human beings in the relationship. An even worse problem is when you start comparing each other to other people you want your partner to be like, this can come across as completely degrading a person. Always respect who you are as a couple and focus on the best parts that make you great.

Next is something surprisingly difficult and something that can instantly cause issues that never existed before in a relationship. That is simply accepting when one is wrong, which is not easier said than done sometimes in couples. Have you ever wondered why it's so easy for children to apologize or accept when they have done something wrong? It's because as we get older and move towards adulthood, we develop our values and ethics, and accepting when wrong can sometimes go against these two prominent points in our life. We don't realize that apologizing, actually, is a prideful thing to do and provides closure to all people involved in the apology. Saying sorry is a simple fee act that can have a hugely positive effect on the person it's directed at.

NO ONE IS PERFECT

You are a human being and that means you will always make mistakes and that is part of the constant learning process in life. There is no such thing as the perfect couple, and all couples go through their own rough patches and tough times that test the relationship at some point. There are things that you find logical that your partner does not, but that does not mean your thinking is superior; it just means your partner looks at the world a bit differently than you. If you are a couple who has this idea of perfecting a relationship, you will only find more problems and become hypocritical of each other even more. You start putting each other on a pedestal that is not truthful and realistic to who you are. You are also not in a relationship to turn your partner into the perfect human being; you are there to help them achieve their best selves.

However, when it comes to apologizing to your partner that is almost a near-perfect thing to do. The feeling of closure from an apology is uplifting and you can probably describe it as an imperfect but perfect act from one human to another. You are correcting a mistake because you are not perfect and perfecting it by admitting to that mistake.

SOME PEOPLE APOLOGIZE DIFFERENTLY

Not everyone apologizes by saying sorry. Some use other ways such as love and affection or spoiling a person as a forgiveness gift. The act of saying sorry can be difficult for some people in terms of pride, but the act of redeeming themselves by bringing happiness to that person is easier. This is something you will quickly find out in a relationship, and honestly, it should be the thought that counts. Some people appreciate the closure of an apology, but sometimes you might have to compromise for the sake of the relationship, especially for simple acts. This is just part of the process as a couple on the road to understanding each other, and it's perfectly normal. This kind of point is common when couples are seeking ways to solve problems they are going through. You might be finding it difficult to find a way to apologize to your partner and they might be doing the same thing; it's a realistic possible scenario. Thus, this causes frustration because neither seems to be accepting the responsibility for your wrongdoings.

An example we can use for this point is if you are dating or married to someone who is quiet and not the most talkative person. It can sometimes be difficult for them to verbally apologize. However, they take you out to your favorite place or make you your favorite food as a way of apologizing. It's then your duty as a partner to acknowledge that apology even though they did not actually say the words. This just builds the understanding and bond in a relationship, and down the line gives them the confidence to just say it, but your partner spoiling you as a sign of apology is good too. Though, they should never only spoil you as a sign of apology because that just makes things frustrating and materialistic.

FOCUS ON THE GOOD

When you start comparing each other to other people, you stop focusing on the good about each other and what you have to positively offer the relationship. You may even forget the good about each other completely, and this will only send your relationship on a downward trajectory. Other than that, comparing each other can create severe resentment and jealousy that may never be able to be reversed. Always focus on the positive aspects of your relationship, because in times of crisis, it's what you will use to keep the relationship going and strong. To get the relationship back to its best, you are usually asked questions such as "What is good about your relationship?" "What is the best thing about your partner?" "What do you wish you had back in the relationship?" or "What things did you do together that made you happy?" All of these questions are used to associate each other with positivity in a situation that has become negative.

You focus on the reasons why you got into a relationship and what are indeed the best parts about it. One of the best ways to do this is to retrace your steps back to the beginning of your relationship. Many couples are afraid to admit that some of their best times were at the start of their relationship. You may even shock yourself with some of the things you did just to get the attention of your partner, so it's a good idea to reminisce about these things together.

GIVE EACH OTHER TIME

Time is something you have regularly read by now as a solution for many romantic relationships problems, and that's because it's a universal application for solving problems. Giving someone time also means you don't have to directly get involved in the conflict, allowing you and your partner to individually think. Giving yourself or your partner time is often important when you are trying to decide if you were wrong about something, and it gives you a way of working on an apology. If you are two strong-minded opinionated individuals, this is often the best solution to coming up with an apology. If you are a person who doesn't like to admit when you are wrong, sometimes you just need time to think about it and swallow your pride.

This may seem childish and immature, but it's a reality that people struggle to figure out why they are wrong.

Have you ever been in a situation where someone is wrong, and they try to justify why they are not? Well, you could be in a relationship with someone like that, so that's something to think about. Remember, don't communicate it to your partner as if it's childish or immature. Respect the fact that it's just the way of understanding a situation, and in time they will come around to apologize. Lastly, if you have given your partner a long time to apologize for something and they don't seem to be interested, let them know politely that you need closure for something that has been bothering you. Sometimes all someone needs is a little bit of closure, and this prevents you from carrying grudges against your partner.

YOU CAN ASK FOR HELP COLLECTIVELY

When it comes to comparing each other to other people and couples, you may not ever actually ask, or approach said person or couple. Though instead of comparing, why not ask the couple what they do to maintain that happiness in parts of your relationship you are struggling in. It's never a bad idea to ask other couples—especially more experienced ones—what they do to keep the relationship strong and happy. Other happy couples you know are living breathing examples of what you need to do to get your relationship back on track, so there really is no harm in asking them for advice. One important thing to note is that you should talk to these couples as a collective and not necessarily by yourself. All members in the relationship should be present, so you have multiple ideas and opinions and can sort of brainstorm solutions. This is also something you should not feel embarrassed to do as long as your mindset is that you are trying to improve your relationship.

Also, the couple you are admiring should also be one that is willing to help because they should have no reason to give you bad advice. You can think of it as like when you ask your parents for advice as a kid because they are more experienced individuals. They may have been through the crisis or problems you might be currently going through or expecting. Be sure not to disclose too much and always ask questions. This couple is not there as your therapists, they are just there to give you simple advice; whether you use it or not is up to you.

SUMMARY

It's normal once in a while to look at other happy couples when you are going through your own couple crisis. Understand that they may share a totally different type of relationship to yours and they are most likely going through issues of their own, but just handling it better. The biggest problem though to take from this chapter is the resentment and jealousy caused by comparing one another to something unrealistic or not who you are. This can be irreversible damage that can lead to actual hatred for each other and can individually create self-doubt. Always do your best to focus on the good about yourself and the good about your partner, then find your equilibrium for each other. You can also retrace your steps as to how your relationship became a comparing contest, to begin with. Focusing on the good prevents self-doubt and any shred of doubt you may have about your partner. After all, you are in a mutual relationship together.

As always, give each other time to figure out what is the next step of your relationship. Time away from each other may give you the necessary reflection about the good in your relationship and motivate you to make it work. When you were together you were seeing the negative, but now that you are separate, you see the reasons why you should be together. Lastly, if you admire another couple so much and want to know how they are so happy, you can just ask them. They have no reason to give you bad advice and you can choose whether that advice is suitable for your relationship. This type of advice costs you nothing and gives you a different perspective from completely neutral opinions. However, make sure you do these things together; try not to go behind your partner's back and ask for advice together. By going together, you are collectively agreeing that there is an issue and giving the couple you are asking the impression that you are really serious about what they do to succeed in their relationship.

Chapter 9
COUPLE GOALS

"Love is a promise, love is a souvenir, once given never forgotten, never let it disappear" (John Lennon).

It's essential to have collective goals as a couple. It shows that you value the relationship together and it provides the necessary motivation to do something together. You establish couple goals mainly to have a joint agreement on something the both of you want to achieve or improve in your relationship. Almost every happy couple you meet has some sort of short and/or long-term goals they are trying to achieve together. They may not always be successful in achieving them, but they go through that shared failure.

Couple goals also create equality in a relationship because each person has to put the same amount of effort, otherwise, it won't be achieved. One of the best feelings you can have as a couple is when you achieve something together regardless of the significance. It strengthens the relationship and motivates each other to do well and brings that good feel factor and helps you realize that you are with the right person. Another big reason for setting goals is it prevents laziness and provides a bit of healthy pressure to work hard for each other. The word "couple" itself represents two, so it's important you stick to that.

IMPORTANCE OF SETTING GOALS

When setting goals for each other, it's important that they are realistic for the situation you are in and where you want to be or achieve. Don't set unrealistic goals for each other for your relationship. As much as it's okay to fail together, don't set yourselves up for failure from the get-go. Unrealistic goals should stay as dreams for your relationship until there comes a point when you can realistically achieve them. Having dreams is different from having goals. You may have a shared dream of what you want to achieve in years to come, but you have goals as stepping stones to achieve those dreams. Understand the capabilities of your partner when setting goals as well as any individual goals they might have. There might be things they are prioritizing for themselves as an individual, and it's important that you respect that. Communicate with each other about where you see yourself in a particular time period and convert that to a goal that you can work towards as a team without compromising your own individual goals in the process. However, there might be a scenario where your individual goals cross paths with your couple goals. In this case, you just need to sit down as a couple and reassess how to achieve the goals.

Try to stick to a deadline when setting goals together so you don't have to extend it all the time. The reason is you don't want to start procrastinating about achieving something. If you do set a deadline for your goals and don't achieve it, be sure not to pass the blame over to your partner. Express the failure together in a constructive manner, reassess your capabilities as a couple and tweak the goal(s) where necessary. Don't be embarrassed if you make them easier. You are just being realistic and there is always the possibility you can over-achieve. You also cannot account for everything when you're going for a joint goal. There are external factors such as your health, family, friends, house, job, etc. that may present unforeseen obstacles. So, what are the usual types of goals you need to set as a couple?

Goal 1: Financial and Material Goals

Firstly, you have financial and material goals, which are all the achievements and objectives you set as a couple around your monetary means of life. There might be a certain holiday destination the two of you can't afford now but want to work towards. There might be a possible promotion opportunity at work. You have identified possible investment opportunities or want to start a business together. Financial and material goals as a couple require a certain amount of trust. It's sometimes difficult to be the one in a relationship that is not earning as well as the other. If this is the case, it's good to reassure each other that financial circumstances are not going to define the success of the relationship.

Setting financial and material goals together can be tricky because money is involved and it's something you jointly want to achieve. Financial and material goals are also not necessarily long-term or short-term, it depends on the financial situation of your relationship. Therefore, when setting these types of goals, try not to make it something too over the top and rather strive to achieve something tangible. For example, this tangible goal could be a new car for you to share, and it does not necessarily have to be an expensive car. What this does is broaden your financial/material goal of getting a new car whether it's a Ferrari or a Ford Fiesta. The achievement was made together.

With regard to material goals, make sure you don't become a couple whose happiness revolves around materialistic things, especially if success comes your way. Always stay grounded and humble. Don't turn into completely different people and disassociate yourselves from those who stuck with you when you had nothing at some point. Yes, celebrate your goal achievements, you earned it, though keep a strong head on both shoulders, and if one of you steps out of that boundary, let each other know. Don't forget to share your achievements and not necessarily your wealth. It's still important to have "what's yours is yours" and "what's mine is mine" in the back of your mind just to maintain your own independence.

Goal 2: Shared Knowledge

When setting goals, always share knowledge with one another because you might know more about something or know something your partner did not know at all. Withholding knowledge from your partner is selfish and not in the best interest of the relationship. You want your partner to achieve their goals, and if you can help them, then share that knowledge with them. You can possibly even make that individual goal a joint goal. Communicating and sharing knowledge as a couple is also a good bonding technique.

Teaching each other new things creates intimate interaction and are experiences you will never forget. Have you ever been in a situation where your partner has taught you something? Did you ever forget that experience? That's a connection unique only to couples and is a permanent imprint that someone never forgets. Throughout all the relationships you might have gone through to where you are now, you remember the lessons you learned from them right? Even if they were negative lessons, you never forget them and adjust accordingly to the next relationship. The knowledge that you have now can be used to improve your next or current relationship without even realizing it.

Goal 3: Making Promises

When you make a promise to someone, it's an unbreakable goal that you give to someone that must be achieved at some point in time. Depending on your morals and ethics, promising someone something means asking them to place their full trust in you with regard to achieving said goal. However, it's always easier to make joint promises in a relationship and is also dependent on how seriously you take it. Some people change the way they view you by the promises you keep, and it sometimes only takes one failed promise for them to permanently few you in a certain way.

The idea is to never make promises to someone unless you are 100% sure you are going to achieve them. For example, one of you has a drinking problem and you make a promise to your partner that you will lessen your consumption of alcohol. This can be regarded as a lifetime promise and is a couple of goals between the two of you in which you agree that you will not drink as much as you used to. You turn this into a goal by seeing the annual progress of your partner or even the both of you in wanting to curb the amount of drinking you do. Promises can therefore be defined as progressive goals you set for yourself and trusted goals you set for your partner together.

Goal 4: Couples Team Building

By now you understand that couple goals are based around only teamwork and are separate from your individual goals unless you choose to include them. Though teamwork is also the motivation for picking up your partner when you see them failing. You want to equally achieve a goal together but every now and then you may need to pick up the slack because your partner is struggling for many reasons. They may have family responsibilities that require their attention temporarily, their health might be a concern, or they are lacking motivation through difficulties that could be emotional, physical, or financial.

It won't always be smooth sailing, so sometimes you have to help them, and the same goes for you when you are going through the same thing. This is the essence of couple team building, this provides the foundations of physical, mental, and emotional strength that you have each other's back no matter the scenario if you are in something together.

Goal 5: Love and Support

When you are striving to achieve something together, there should be no shred of negativity along the way to that goal. A couple of goals are positive objectives you set for the improvement of your relationship, so there should be nothing to be negative about. You should never pass the blame when a goal is failed, but rather applaud the effort and try again together. You should never set goals that are serious enough to end your relationship; that's unnecessary pressure you don't need as a couple. There should be love and support even in failure because it's the only way you will progress as a couple.

If you become negative every time you fail, it will also spill off into your individual goal and finally blow over into your overall relationship negatively. In fact, the best time to show love and support is when you fail. It provides the necessary conduit for motivation and to try again for the same goal. You can call it a "couple comeback," where you are persistent in achieving something you failed together. Always spread love and show support before, during, and after the goal no matter the results.

SUMMARY

Couple goals are staple realistic objectives every single couple needs to have. If you look at how you were just before you made your relationship official, your goal might have been to date each other. Goals give us the motivation and purpose to strive for something a bit bigger than ourselves. It also gives us the necessary failure to learn about our capabilities and what we need to do to improve as a whole. Thus, this makes the importance of setting couples goals paramount because it's the necessary motivation and drive to keep the relationship as well as improve it wherever possible if necessary. The first goal was financial and material goals, which is to basically set realistic goals of where you jointly want to be or even go.

These are the luxury goals created to enjoy your lives outside the relationship and explore new things together. Your relationship gets stronger because your progression is happening equally. The second thing that was mentioned was shared knowledge. You share what you know and your partner shares what they know. One of you in the relationship might be more financially smart and the other might be more practically smart; you have a goal to achieve and both of you focus on the parts you are good at.

The next is making promises. These are usually lifetime commitments you or your partner makes concerning the relationship. You take these promises and shorten them into parts to create goals and prove yourself individually and for the sake of keeping your relationship. Always remember to never make a promise you will never be able to keep; it can seriously damage a couple's relationship permanently. You then have a couple's team building. The basic purpose of this goal is to always pick up after each other when the other is struggling.

If your partner is dealing with some sort of crisis, it's your responsibility to support them through it and help them out where you can. Lastly, this follows love and support. Even though you may pick up after your partner and possibly fail the goal, you don't need to blame them for it. Rather love and support them because they will also know that they may have not played their part the way they wanted to. Regardless of whether you achieve a goal or not, the final outcome should always be the love and support for each other at all times.

The idea of couple goals is to find your strengths and weaknesses without causing issues in your relationship. If you are having trouble in your relationship, setting a couple of goals could well be the path to identifying the reasons why. Overall, the golden rule of this chapter is putting in the effort and working together to achieve a common objective as a couple only. Don't at any point involve other people, friends, or family even if you are really tempted to. You are doing this because you and your partner are having difficulties working together, so use that as a solid motivator when moving forward.

Chapter 10
EXERCISES AND QUESTIONS TO PROMOTE A HEALTHY RELATIONSHIP

"It takes two to speak the truth: one to speak and another to hear"

(Henry David Thoreau).

The focus of this chapter is to provide you with a guide that you can use to deepen your connection with your partner. With the help of these questions and exercises, you will be able to learn more about one another and talk openly about the topics that are most important for maintaining a great relationship. Use them to bond with one another and watch your relationship thrive.

Four rules for getting the most out of these conversations:

Work with your partner to find a solution.

Listen without judging.

Give full attention to your partner's words. Turn off the television, and the phone, and make intense and sincere eye contact.

Your partner's answers contain the solution. Write the answer to each question, and after your partner has finished, ask each other questions. Take notes on your partner's answers; they contain clear indications on how to improve your relationship already today.

CONNECTION

- Write down three things that you and your partner think you have in common.

Compare your respective answers.

- What did you think the first time you saw your partner?

- Do you remember a moment or situation where you wanted to apologize to your partner, but you didn't? If yes, why didn't you do it?

- Write your personal problem and ask advice from your partner about how you handle it.

- Do you have a set goal for this year? If yes, can your partner help you in any way?

- Where do you see us five years from now?

- Is there anything I could do for you that I'm not already doing?

- What was the first thing you noticed about me today?

- If you could change one thing about me,
what would you change?

- When we spend time together, what do you enjoy doing?

- What was the one thing that drew you to me in the beginning?

MONICA TRAVIS

- When did you know that you were in love with me?

- What was your favorite part of our first date?

- How much do you care about what other people think of our relationship?

- What is your favorite memory that we have shared?

- Is there anything that you wish we could do as a couple?

- Are you happy with our daily routine?

Discovery

- Tell your partner the story of your life, starting from your first memory and moving forward in as much detail as possible, including everything you remember that your partner still doesn't know.

- What is the strangest food or drink you've ever tasted?

- What's the craziest thing you've ever done?

- Share with your partner an embarrassing moment in your life.

- What are the three things in your life that you feel most grateful for?

- What's the funniest thing your parents would tell your partner about you when you were a kid?

- How do you spend your time when you're not with your partner?

- What are your top three things that are really important to you in life?

- Describe in detail what your "perfect" day should be from morning to night.

- As a man/woman, what would you say that your biggest desire is?

- What is the one thing you enjoy doing the most?

- If you could take up one new hobby, what would it be?

- If you weren't on the career path you are now, what would you change?

- Do you feel that you spend enough time with your friends?

- If you could teach me anything, what would it be?

- What is one thing that relaxes you most?

- When you are angry, what calms you down?

- Where is one place you'd like to go with me?

- What is your idea of the perfect evening?

- What is your favorite restaurant right now?

- In what ways are we similar? In what ways are we different?

Intimacy

- Is there something you would like to try?

- What is your favorite position?

- What is the first physical quality you notice about me?

- What is something you desire most in the bedroom?

- Are there any fantasies that you'd like to bring to life?

- Do you feel like you are getting enough excitement in the bedroom?

- When did we have our best sex?

- Is there anything that I am neglecting in the bedroom?

- What is something that could make our intimacy better?

- How does my touch make you feel?

- If you could do anything to me, what would you do?

Exercises

- Reverse your role for 7 days.

List your respective family responsibilities precisely (cooking, cleaning the house, accompanying children to school, throwing garbage, etc.).

- Plan a week together where you can do each other's family activities. This exercise will help you better appreciate what you do for each other.

- List below three possible interests or recreational activities that you could share with your partner (examples: outdoor sports, cooking class, dance course, foreign language course).

- Which of these interests would you most like to do together?

- Establish a date in the next month and start this new activity together.

- Give your partner a sincere compliment daily for 30 days.

- Write down a few new places you'd like to visit or activities you'd like to try. Each piece of paper should contain one. Mix them up in a jar and take turns selecting one on date night. This will allow you to branch out of your comfort zones while doing the things that you have each been wanting to experience. Make sure that you put in the effort to have a date night regularly. This will show your partner that you are serious about keeping the relationship exciting and fun.

- If something has been bothering you for a while and you can feel the tension building, sit across from one another in a quiet room. Look into one another's eyes and just breathe for a few seconds. Before you begin speaking, smile until your partner smiles back. This exercise will allow you to gather your thoughts and spark the connection that you share. Thinking before speaking is the best way to prevent saying something out of anger that you will regret.

- Have a competition throughout the day and see who can say or send the most compliments. After you both get home, tally up the results. The winner gets to do whatever they want to the loser in the bedroom. With the excitement of the prize and the sparks flying from all of the compliments given, this game will definitely allow you to reconnect in an exciting way.

- When you are having a disagreement, use a pillow or another object to signify who gets to talk. By making sure that you are not talking over each other or interrupting each other, both of you will be able to get your individual points across. The person holding the item should be allowed to fully explain themselves before passing it over. By practicing self-discipline, both of you will be able to feel that you are being heard.

- While you are out in public together, take a look at the other couples around you and give them backstories. Imagine how they met and how long they have been together, the more detailed the better. Before long, you will both be laughing to yourselves about this private moment that you are sharing while feeling that bond grow even more. Being able to laugh together is one thing that will bring you closer as a couple.

Chapter 11
40 QUIZZES TO DEVELOP A DEEPER EMOTIONAL AND PHYSICAL INTIMACY

THE MATCH GAME

This is a quiz to see how well you know one another. Both of you get to read the questions and pen your own answers in private. At the end of the game, you will both reveal your answers to each question at the same time. Each match earns you one point.

Points scale:

1–4: Try getting to know each other on a deeper level!

5–7: You know a decent amount about one another, but there is still more to learn!

8–10: You know each other very well!

1. Where did the two of you go on your first date?
2. When is your anniversary?
3. Who is your partner's favorite musician?
4. Where would your partner love to vacation?

5. Describe your partner's favorite meal.

6. If your partner had a choice, what kind of car would they drive?

7. Who is your partner's best friend?

8. How many siblings does your partner have?

9. Name a fun memory that the two of you shared recently.

10. What is your partner's career goal?

THE BEDROOM QUIZ

This quiz focuses on likes/dislikes in the bedroom. Give yourself one point for each correct answer you get.

Points scale:

1–10: You need to focus on your partner's needs more.

11–15: You have a nice level of intimacy, but there is more to uncover.

16–20: Your intimacy is higher than average!

1. Does your partner prefer intimacy in the morning or at night?
2. What is one thing that is off-limits?
3. What is your partner's biggest turn-on?
4. Ideally, how often does your partner want to have sex?
5. Is being in public a turn-on?
6. Would you ever engage in a threesome?
7. Bed or couch?
8. Lights on or lights off?
9. What is one thing you have yet to try but want to?
10. What is your partner's favorite body part on you?
11. What is your partner's favorite position?

12. How do you know when your partner is enjoying something?

13. How important is intimacy in your relationship?

14. Does your partner desire more intimacy?

15. What was the last fantasy you acted out as a couple?

16. What is an upcoming fantasy that you are excited to act out?

17. Does your partner have any kinks? If so, name them.

18. Is using toys a turn-on?

19. Does your partner enjoy roleplaying?

20. What is one sure way to take your partner to the next level in bed?

DEAL OR NO DEAL

Each answer will be yes or no. For each yes, you have a deal. For each no, you do not earn a point.

Points scale:

1–2: No deal—try again!

3–4: Deal! You know a little bit about one another.

4–5: Deal with the potential for more deals! Your intimacy is growing.

1. Your partner enjoys rough play.
2. Your partner likes it with the lights on.
3. Your partner is more dominant.
4. Your partner wants more sex.
5. Your partner is turned on easily.

HOW DO YOU LOVE? PHYSICAL INTIMACY

Everyone has a unique way they express their love, but which one is yours? This quiz revolves around the topic of physical intimacy.

Points scale:

1–2: You do not show your love through physical intimacy.

3–4: You might show your love through physical intimacy.

4–5: You definitely show your love through physical intimacy.

1. Do you always enjoy cuddling?
2. Do you love to kiss your partner?
3. Do you always hold hands in public?
4. Does your partner's touch soothe you?
5. Is touching important in your relationship?

HOW DO YOU LOVE? ENCOURAGING WORDS

Everyone has a unique way they express their love, but which one is yours? This quiz revolves around the topic of encouraging words.

Points scale:

1–2: You do not use encouraging words to show your love.

3–4: You might use encouraging words to show your love.

4–5: You definitely use encouraging words to show your love.

1. Do you enjoy compliments from your partner?
2. Do you gain reassurance when your partner approves of you?
3. Do you respond well to positive reinforcement?
4. Do you often seek verbal praise?
5. Do you like hearing your partner tell you that they love you?

HOW DO YOU LOVE? A HELPING HAND

Everyone has a unique way they express their love, but which one is yours? This quiz revolves around the topic of offering a helping hand.

Points scale:

1–2: You do not show your love by offering a helping hand.

3–4: You might show your love by offering a helping hand.

4–5: You definitely show your love by offering a helping hand.

1. Does your partner appreciate it when you do the chores?
2. Does it make you feel good when you help your partner?
3. Do you like completing tasks with your partner?
4. Do kind actions go a long way for you?
5. Do you enjoy it when your partner does something without being asked?

HOW DO YOU LOVE? ALONE TIME

Everyone has a unique way they express their love, but which one is yours? This quiz revolves around the topic of having alone time with your partner.

Points scale:

1–2: You do not express your love through alone time.

3–4: You might express your love through alone time.

4–5: You definitely express your love through alone time.

1. Do you love staying in with your partner?
2. Do you enjoy attention from your partner?
3. Do you often feel more important when your partner spends time with you?
4. Do you wish that you had more alone time with your partner?
5. Do you prefer to do fun things with your partner rather than alone or with friends?

HOW DO YOU LOVE? MAKING PURCHASES

Everyone has a unique way of expressing their love, but which one is yours? This quiz revolves around the topic of purchasing gifts.

Points scale:

1–2: You do not purchase gifts to show your love.

3–4: You might purchase gifts to show your love.

4–5: You definitely purchase gifts to show your love.

1. Do you feel loved when you receive a gift from your partner?
2. Do you enjoy giving your partner gifts?
3. Is gift-giving the equivalent of showing love?
4. Do you enjoy shopping for your partner?
5. Does receiving a gift make you feel excited?

ARE YOU PASSIONATE?

Find out if you are a passionate couple! You get one point for every "YES" answer.

Points scale:

1–3: Your relationship isn't very passionate.

4–6: You have some passion in your relationship.

7–10: Your relationship is passionate!

1. Do you have sex often?
2. Are you touchy-feely with your partner?
3. Do you hold hands in public?
4. Do you kiss in public?
5. Is intimacy important to you?
6. Do you both like to try new things in the bedroom?
7. Do you feel satisfied after you have sex?
8. Do you share a lot in common?
9. Is your relationship still growing?
10. Does your heart race while with your partner?

WHICH KINK SHOULD YOU TRY IN THE BEDROOM?

Each "YES" answer will give you a point! Use the scale below to determine which kink you should try as a couple.

Points scale:

1–2: Spanking

3–4: Roleplaying

5: Role reversal

1. Would you describe your sex as "vanilla?"
2. Do you have a set schedule?
3. Do you have enough sex?
4. Have you tried something new lately?
5. Do you consider yourselves to be kinky?

IS ROMANCE ALIVE IN YOUR RELATIONSHIP?

Assess your current relationship by giving yourself a point for each of these statements you can relate to as a couple.

Points scale:

1–2: Your relationship needs work.

3–4: You have some romance present.

5: The romance is alive and kicking!

1. You get physically excited when you see your partner.
2. You would consider your relationship more romantic than average.
3. You often touch one another, even in non-sexual ways.
4. You feel completely comfortable in the bedroom.
5. You feel satisfied in your relationship.

IS YOUR PARTNER YOUR BEST FRIEND?

Score yourself by giving yourself a point for each relatable statement.

Points scale:

1–2: You need to get to know one another more.

3–4: You two are decently close friends.

5: You are the best of friends!

1. You have fun with your partner.
2. You enjoy spending your free time together.
3. You never get bored at home together.
4. You can tell your partner everything.
5. You feel 100% comfortable when talking with your partner about serious issues.

SHOULD YOU CHANGE YOUR RELATIONSHIP?

Any relationship can become stuck in the same stage. Is it time to change things up? Give yourself a point for every answer you relate to.

Points scale:

1. 1–2: Your relationship is still growing!

3–4: A change would serve you well.

5: Change something soon for the sake of your happiness.

2. You do not know what to talk about with your partner.
3. You have stopped having sex.
4. You feel like you are at a dead-end in your relationship.
5. Other couples seem happier.
6. You wish things were more like the movies.

HOW TO IMPROVE YOUR RELATIONSHIP

It can be hard knowing what to do next. This quiz will help. Give yourself a point for each "YES" answer.

Points scale:

1–2: Go on more dates.

3–4: Talk to each other more.

5: Have more sex.

1. Do you not spend enough quality time together?
2. Do you feel out of the loop with your partner?
3. Do you bicker or argue a lot?
4. Did you feel happier in the past?
5. Do you often wish that you had more passion?

IS YOUR INTIMACY ENOUGH?

Give yourself a point for each "YES" answer.

Points scale:

1–2: You need more intimacy in your relationship.

3–4: Your level of intimacy is okay.

5: You share great intimate moments!

1. Do you feel like your partner is your soul mate?
2. Does your partner know how to please you?
3. Can you enjoy spending time together without having sex?
4. Do you see yourself growing old together?
5. Do your friends and family support your relationship?

DO YOU TRUST YOUR PARTNER?

Give yourself a point for each "TRUE" answer you have.

Points scale:

1–2: There is almost no trust in your relationship—work on facilitating it!

3–4: You trust your partner, but you have doubts sometimes.

5: The trust levels are great in your relationship.

1. You have never checked your partner's phone secretly.
2. When your partner is at work, you believe them.
3. You do not feel anxious when your partner hangs out with friends.
4. You have never felt your partner was lying to you.
5. You believe your partner because they have never given you a reason not to.

WILL YOU BE TOGETHER FOREVER?

Give yourself a point for each "YES" answers your select.

Points scale:

1–3: Your relationship is fragile right now; it could use work.

4–6: The two of you are pretty strong but can be stronger.

7–10: You are soul mates!

1. Can you see yourself with your partner in 10 years?
2. Are you happy with the course of your relationship?
3. Are your needs met?
4. Do you feel satisfied in the bedroom?
5. Do you know how to get through arguments successfully?
6. Do you communicate and speak your whole mind?
7. Are you able to talk about anything together?
8. Do you have fun together outside of the bedroom?
9. Do your friends and family think you two are a good match?
10. Do you feel that you are in a healthy relationship?

ARE YOU AND YOUR PARTNER A GOOD MATCH?

Take this quiz to determine your compatibility as a couple. Give yourself a point for every "YES" answer.

1–3: You might not be a good match.

4–6: The two of you are decently matched with room for improvement.

7–10: You are a stellar match!

1. You often know what your partner is thinking.
2. You have a good grasp of your partner's feelings.
3. Your partner does things for you without you asking.
4. You feel loved and cared about at all times.
5. You feel that your partner puts you first.
6. You think your relationship is a priority to your partner.
7. You can say that you are honestly happy.
8. You want to spend the rest of your life with your partner.
9. You have a lot in common.
10. You always have something to talk about.

IS YOUR RELATIONSHIP HEALTHY?

Give yourself a point for each "YES" answer you have.

Points scale:

1–2: Your relationship might be unhealthy—reevaluate the dynamic.

3–4: Your relationship could use more boundaries/respect.

5: This is a healthy relationship!

1. Do you feel respected by your partner?
2. Are you always able to speak your mind?
3. Is "walking on eggshells" a foreign feeling in your relationship?
4. When you argue, can you speak calmly with one another?
5. Do you both agree that your needs are met?

THE FAVORITES QUIZ

Give yourself a point for each correct answer you provide.

Points scale:

1–2: Try again!

3–4: You know each other decently well.

5: You have a true understanding of what your partner enjoys!

1. When is your partner's favorite time to be intimate?
2. What is your partner's favorite position?
3. What is your partner's best sexual memory?
4. What does your partner love most about you?
5. What turns your partner on?

A RANDOM ASSORTMENT

Take this quiz to discover even more about one another. Give yourself a point for each correct answer you provide.

Points scale:

1–3: You did an okay job.

4–6: You did a pretty nice job!

7–10: You share an amazing level of intimacy!

1. Who is your partner's best friend?
2. What is your partner's career goal?
3. Does your partner enjoy surprises?
4. Name one of your partner's favorite TV shows.
5. Can your partner whistle?
6. What is your partner's love language?
7. If your partner could eat one meal forever, what would it be?
8. Does your partner enjoy road trips?
9. What is your partner's biggest pet peeve?
10. Is your partner kinky?

ARE YOU AN INTROVERTED COUPLE?

Find out if the two of you are introverts! Give yourself a point for each "YES" answer.

Points scale:

1–2: Not very introverted

3–4: Pretty introverted

5: Introverted, no doubt

1. Your love language is quality time.
2. You both enjoy staying in and watching movies.
3. You prefer to be alone with your partner than in public.
4. You two have more fun when no one else is around.
5. You would choose to spend time with your partner in a one-on-one setting rather than on a group date.

ARE YOU AN EXTROVERTED COUPLE?

Find out if the two of you are extroverts! Give yourself a point for each "YES" answer.

Points scale:

1–2: Not very extroverted

3–4: Pretty extroverted

5: Extroverted, no doubt

1. You love hanging out with other couples.
2. You host people regularly.
3. You love to get into banters in a group setting.
4. The two of you have a lot of friends.
5. You are both known for being the life of the party.

THE CONFLICT RESOLUTION QUIZ

Find out how well the two of you resolve conflict. Give yourself a point for each "YES" answer.

Points scale:

1–2: Needs improvement.

3–4: You handle conflict decently well.

5: You are masters at handling conflict!

1. When you get into an argument, you can usually let it go.
2. After a fight, you do not feel any lingering anger.
3. You know how to calm your partner down.
4. You can communicate without yelling at each other.
5. You know how to agree to disagree.

DO YOU APPRECIATE YOUR PARTNER ENOUGH?

Find out how appreciative you are! Give yourself a point for each "YES" answer.

Points scale:

1–3: You need to do more.

4–6: You are doing a great job.

7–10: Your partner feels 100% loved and appreciated by you!

1. You know how to say "I love you" without saying the words.
2. You understand what your partner needs at all times.
3. If your partner is worried, you know how to calm them down.
4. You know what presses their buttons.
5. You compliment your partner often.
6. Your partner has told you recently that they feel appreciated.
7. You feel that you have grown with your partner.
8. You consider your partner your best friend.
9. You feel like your partner adds amazing qualities to your life.
10. You have gotten your partner a gift just because.

DO YOU MAKE YOUR PARTNER HAPPY?

Give yourself a point for every "YES" answer you provide.

Points scale:

1–3: You could do more…

4–6: Your partner is pretty happy.

7–10: You are great at making your partner happy!

1. Your partner laughs with you a lot.
2. You know how to be there when they are crying.
3. You feel comfortable talking about all emotions/feelings.
4. You know your partner's gift preferences.
5. You take your partner out on dates.
6. You satisfy your partner in the bedroom.
7. You understand your partner's needs.
8. You know how to grow with your partner.
9. Your partner loves spending time with you.
10. You are continuing to make memories with your partner.

WHAT SHOULD YOU ADD TO YOUR RELATIONSHIP?

Find out now! Give yourself a point for each "YES" answer you provide.

Points scale:

1–3: More date nights

4–6: More quality time

7–10: More sex

1. You often run out of ideas for what to do together.
2. You do not have many things in common right now.
3. You wish your partner did something differently.
4. You hope that your relationship will become more passionate.
5. You miss the spark you once had with your partner.
6. You are no longer in the honeymoon stage.
7. You are feeling restless in the relationship.
8. You do not understand your partner's desires.
9. You have not changed the routine in a while.
10. You feel like your relationship can be boring.

ARE YOU COUPLE GOALS?

Take this quiz to find out if other couples envy the connection that you share! Give yourself a point for every "YES" answer you provide.

Points scale:

1–3: Your relationship could use some work.

4–6: Your relationship is pretty great.

7–10: Your relationship is a couple of goals!

1. You can turn any situation into a romantic one.
2. You still give each other butterflies.
3. You are both comfortable hanging out with other couples.
4. You happily spend time together and apart.
5. You have trust for one another.
6. You know how to apologize to each other.
7. You are willing to go the extra mile for your partner.
8. You both excel at gift-giving.
9. You celebrate anniversaries and special dates.
10. You both willingly work on the relationship.

HOW CAN YOU HELP YOUR RELATIONSHIP GROW?

Every couple wants to continue growing in their relationship. Find out how you can do the same! Give yourself a point for each "YES" answer you provide.

Points scale:

1–7: Get to know each other on a deeper level.

8–14: Work on your conflict resolution skills.

15–20: Continue loving and respecting one another openly.

1. You currently feel stuck.
2. You can clearly see your partner in your future.
3. You have always known that the two of you were meant to be.
4. You fight a lot.
5. You sometimes do not understand one another.
6. You both have a lot to work on personally.
7. You can work together to solve problems.
8. You feel invincible when you are with your partner.
9. Others comment on your connection.
10. You do not understand your partner when they get upset.
11. Your partner knows you better than anyone.

12. Together, you are better.
13. Many people want what you two have.
14. You have considered breaking up.
15. You have gone on a break from the relationship.
16. When you have a problem, you let your partner know.
17. You do not keep secrets from your partner.
18. You understand what your downfalls are as a couple.
19. You are fascinated by your partner.
20. There is nobody else you would rather be with.

HOW GREAT ARE YOU AT BEING IN A RELATIONSHIP?

Find out how well you are doing as a significant other! Give yourself a point for each "YES" answer you provide.

Points scale:

1–2: You are not a great partner right now.

3–4: Your skills could use improvement.

5: You are the ultimate partner!

1. You love and accept your partner.
2. You see their flaws as positive traits that you accept.
3. You understand what your partner says to you.
4. You love to see your partner happy.
5. You are willing to make compromises.

ARE YOUR COMMUNICATION SKILLS GOOD ENOUGH?

Communication is essential—find out now. Give yourself a point for each "YES" answer you provide.

Points scale:

1–2: Could use improvement

3–4: Decent communication skills

5: Superb communication skills

1. You maintain eye contact with your partner while speaking.
2. You pick up on their non-verbal cues.
3. You know the right words to say.
4. You know how to apologize properly.
5. You understand what makes your partner happy.

CAN YOU HANDLE YOUR JEALOUSY?

Jealousy can get the best of everyone. Find out if yours is under control. Give yourself a point for each "YES" answer you provide.

Points scale:

1–2: You need to work on your insecurities.

3–4: You mostly trust your partner.

5: You have a healthy way of managing your jealousy!

1. You trust your partner to hang out with others while you are not around.
2. You do not worry about your partner's exes.
3. You never go through your partner's phone when they are not in the room.
4. You take their word for what it is.
5. You are genuinely secure in your relationship.

DO YOU BELIEVE THAT YOUR PARTNER FINDS YOU ATTRACTIVE?

Make sure that your self-confidence levels are high enough! Give yourself a point for each "YES" answer you provide.

Points scale:

1–2: Your insecurities get the best of you.

3–4: You are pretty secure in your feelings.

5: You believe your partner 100%!

1. When your partner compliments you, this is truly how they feel about you.
2. You feel comfortable being undressed around them.
3. You do not think they want to be with someone else.
4. You have many positive traits.
5. You know how to be sexy and appealing.

ARE YOU READY FOR KIDS?

Give yourself a point for each "YES" answer you provide.

Points scale:

1–3: You should probably work on yourselves first.

4–6: You would make decent parents right now.

7–10: Yes, have kids together!

1. You both feel that you are not selfish.
2. You are ready to expand your family.
3. You have been wanting kids for a while.
4. You are both in good financial standing.
5. You love taking care of others.
6. You are nurturing to your partner.
7. You feel that you have lived out your dreams already.
8. You have enough space in your house.
9. You are ready to grow your relationship.
10. You have an unbreakable bond with your partner.

SHOULD YOU GET A PET TOGETHER?

Give yourself a point for each "YES" answer you provide.

Points scale:

1–2: Maybe not right now.

3–4: Sure, get a pet.

5: You should definitely get a pet together!

1. You are both responsible.
2. You are both willing to make changes.
3. You both love animals.
4. You both take turns doing housework.
5. You both know how to compromise.

SHOULD YOU SPEND MORE TIME TOGETHER?

Find out now! Give yourself a point for each "YES" answer you provide.

Points scale:

1–2: You spend a decent amount of time together.

3–4: You should spend more time together.

5: You definitely need to spend more time together to help your relationship!

1. You feel like you do not see your partner enough.
2. You wish you had more quality time together.
3. You both work a lot.
4. You usually spend the weekends with friends.
5. You feel like your partner is mysterious at times.

IS THE SEX HOT ENOUGH?

Give yourself a point for each "YES" answer you provide.

Points scale:

1–2: It is pretty good sex.

3–4: The sex is great.

5: You have mind-blowing sex!

1. You and your partner both finish when you have sex.
2. You and your partner try new things.
3. You and your partner are very physically affectionate.
4. You know what turns each other on.
5. You are vocal in the bedroom.

SHOULD YOU KISS MORE?

Find out! Give yourself a point for each "YES" answer you provide.

Points scale:

1–2: You kiss a great amount.

3–4: Kissing more would benefit the relationship.

5: You should absolutely kiss more!

1. You go days without kissing each other.
2. You sometimes skip the goodbye kisses.
3. You are not willing to kiss around other people.
4. Kissing does not usually turn you on.
5. You do not kiss during foreplay that often.

DO YOU TURN YOUR PARTNER ON?

Give yourself a point for each "YES" answer you provide.

Points scale:

1–2: You turn them on a decent amount.

3–4: You really know how to turn them on.

5: The way you turn them on drives them crazy!

1. You always know what your partner needs during sex.
2. You can tell that your partner enjoys sex by their non-verbal communication.
3. You are willing to go the extra mile in the bedroom.
4. Your sex usually lasts for over an hour.
5. You have sex more than three times a week.

WHAT SHOULD YOU DO FOR DATE NIGHT?

Find out now! Give yourself a point for each "YES" answer you provide.

Points scale:

1–2: Watch a movie together.

3–4: Go out for dinner.

5: Take a bubble bath.

>You had a date last week.

>You often try out new places on your dates.

>You love going out with your partner.

>Staying in feels just as exciting to you.

>Your partner makes you feel appreciated.

Conclusion

"You know its love when all you want is that person to be happy, even if you're not part of their happiness"
(Roberts, n.d.).

There are four main focal points every chapter in this book requires from you and your partner. Compromise for each other, love each other, understand each other, and put in the effort for each other. When any one of these is not being done, your relationship will immediately have problems. Compromise where you can. You can't have everything your way in a relationship, and you sometimes have to think about the needs and wants of your partner. Compromising can be difficult because it does not follow your interests, but it means the world to the right person who you are compromising for.

The right partner will never tell you to compromise something that changes who you are because they are with you for who you are. Secondly, love each other even in the times when you hate each other. Why hate each other when there is enough hate in the world already? There are couples out there going through worse problems than you are and still love each other regardless. Love is a free activity that requires little effort other than being there for the person when they need it, otherwise, you may find that person finding it elsewhere—and that is an act they have to deal with.

By incorporating all these factors along with the guides and steps you have learned from this book, it should give you all the tools you need to tackle all your relationship problems. However, if your partner or you have done something quite diabolical or unforgivable, there really is not much you can do to stop them from leaving the relationship. There are no steps on how to get someone back after you have had an affair or maybe had a physical confrontation. This workbook is a guide to help stop you from thinking about having that affair if it crossed your mind and to only entertain the attention of the person you are with.

Also, it's important to note if your partner or you don't want to put in the effort to sort out your issues and you may have explored multiple avenues and worked hard to change their mind and it still does not work, you may need to reconsider whether you or they really want to continue the relationship. As always, communicate and understand what is going through their mind and how they are feeling physically and emotionally. Relationships have very fine lines, and unfortunately, a poorly timed wrong answer or action can have irreversible effects. Use the steps that apply to you in each chapter and adapt them to your own personal situation for the best results. Ask your partner to go through the steps with you and see what might apply to them if you are unsure.

Work together to achieve the goals you set out to get together, embrace the failure, and move on should it happen. Remember to keep your heads and love each other even in situations where it's difficult to. Build on it and make your relationship strong again or in the future. Remember to always refer back to the steps and guides just in case you forgot. This book is designed to last you the entire life cycle of your relationship should maybe you have a few fallouts in between. What makes relationships a thing of utter perfection are in fact the imperfections of each other, imperfect people trying to live the perfect life with each other is a beautiful thing.

Make mistakes make even bigger mistakes, but always make sure that you and your partner always keep the love, support, communication, and commitment to each other and nobody else. Strive to be perfect within each other, as said time and time again as a reminder in this book. Love each other for who you are because that is permanent and that is forever. It's never going to be as smooth sailing and definitely not as easy as you see in the movies. Relationships take hard work in the beginning and should become easier as you grow old together and have fewer responsibilities.

You can't move forward in your relationship if you cannot sit down and make a list of all the things that make your partner happy. Simple small things you need to know, like what is their favorite color? What is their favorite food? What is their worst fear? What is their bad habit? These are some simple questions—that if you don't know about your partner—you need to use and restart your relationship as if it was their first date include a list of these questions and memorize the answers. Lastly and most important, is putting in the work and effort to get your relationship on the right track when you are having problems.

If you don't put in the effort and follow what this book provides you in every chapter at your convenience, what is the point of trying to save your relationship? A successful relationship is between two people putting equal amounts of effort to give their best selves to one another regardless of the good and the bad they encounter. A successful relationship becomes stronger during and after problems, so that when the problem happens again.... Well, is it really a problem anymore? Remember, this workbook is a guide to solving your couple-related problems, ultimately when you get to this chapter, you should have the perfect plan in place to sweep your partner off their feet once again. Good health, good times, good vibes, and good luck to you.

If you liked this book, please let me know your thoughts by leaving a short review on Amazon. Thank you!

References

Gender Stereotyping Quotes. (n.d). Retrieved from https://www.goodreads.com/quotes/tag/gender-stereotypes

Jennifer Aniston Quotes. (n.d.). Retrieved from https://www.goodreads.com/quotes/206094-the-greater-your-capacity-to-love-the-greater-your-capacity

Yasharoff, H. (2018). Sleepless in Seattle 25th Anniversary: 25 Best Quotes from the Rom-com Classic. Retrieved from https://www.usatoday.com/story/life/entertainthis/2018/06/22/sleepless-seattle-25th-anniversary-25-best-lines/719068002/

Inspirational Quotes. (n.d.). Retrieved from

https://www.passiton.com/inspirational-quotes/6569-love-is-that-condition-in-which-the-happiness

Luitjen, S. (n.d.). Inspiring Quotes to Warm Your Heart. Retrieved from https://www.keepinspiring.me/quotes-about-love/

Ziggy Marley Quote. (n.d.). Brainy Quote. Retrieved

from https://www.brainyquote.com/quotes/ziggy_marley_303541

A Quote About Communication. (n.d.). Retrieved from https://jsydsjourney.wordpress.com/2015/03/24/the-way-we-communicate-with-others-and-with-ourselves-ultimately-determines-the-quality-of-our-lives-tony-robbins/

Ma, F. A Julia Robert Quote. Retrieved from https://medium.com/@fredma_43446/you-know-its-love-when-all-you-want-is-that-person-to-be-happy-even-if-you-re-not-part-of-their-71fb4c2977f2

Salmansohn, K. (n.d.). The Minds Journal. Retrieved from https://themindsjournal.com/at-your-absolute-best-you-still-wont-be-good-enough/

A Midsummer Night's Dream. (n.d.). Retrieved from https://www.sparknotes.com/shakespeare/msnd/section1/

Oprah Winfrey Quotes. (n.d.). Retrieved from https://quotefancy.com/quote/879398/Oprah-Winfrey-Don-t-settle-for-a-relationship-that-won-t-let-you-be-yourself

Schwanke, C. (n.d.). 57 Intimate Questions to Ask Your Partner. Retrieved. March 9, 2020, from https://dating.lovetoknow.com/Intimate_Questions_To_Ask_Your_Partner

Printed in Great Britain
by Amazon